From The Women's Press Ltd
12 Ellesmere Road, Bow, London E3 5QX

Alison Fell was born in Scotland and attended Edinburgh Art College. In 1970, when she became involved with women's liberation, she was a housewife and mother in Leeds. Since then she has been active in a number of groups including the Women's Street Theatre Group and women's centres, and has worked on publications including *Ink, Red Rag* and, recently, *Time Out*. She has been a member of the *Spare Rib* collective since 1975 and currently edits the fiction. Her poetry has appeared in the collections *Cutlasses and Earrings* and *Licking the Bed Clean*. She has an eleven-year-old son and lives in London.

Edited and illustrated by
ALISON FELL

Hard Feelings

Fiction and Poetry from Spare Rib

The Women's Press

Published by The Women's Press Limited 1979
A member of the Namara Group
12 Ellesmere Road, Bow, London E3 5QX

Acknowledgement is gratefully made to the authors for permission to reprint their works which were originally published and copyrighted as follows:

'My Death' (copyright © Lynda Schor): 1973

'You, Human Being', a chapter from the novel *You, Human Being* copyright © Marit Paulsen 1972, published by Raben & Sjogren, 1972; published in *Spare Rib* 1974. Translation by Nan Leunbach.

'Her Sweet Jerome' copyright © 1970 by Alice Walker. Reprinted from her volume *In Love and Trouble* by permission of Harcourt Brace Jovanovich Inc.

'too late' (copyright © Astra 1974); 'Uma' by Amiya Rao; 'The Vote' by Margaret Rodriguez; 'Mouselike' by Rosemary Yates: 1975.

'A Week Like Any Other' by Natalia Baranskaya (translation by Pauline Jaray); 'I am a victim' and 'last night when you fell asleep' by Judith Barrington, originally published in *Deviation*, 1975; 'In the Shit No More' by Anya Bostock; 'Nights' by Alison Fell; 'Sensitivity' by Angela Hamblin; 'Tampax', 'Frustruation' and 'Advice' by Frances Landsman; 'Snow White' by the Merseyside Women's Literature Collective; 'O-U-T Spells Out' by Stef Pixner: 1976.

'An Ambivalent Situation' by Gillian Allnutt; 'Mrs Mac and the Witch' by Ros Carne; 'the bath' and 'shout' by Judith Kazantzis; 'The nets' and 'He said: Mostly I feel like a tractor' by Natasha Morgan; 'Bones' by Ann Oosthuizen; 'Eye to Eye' by Tina Reid; 'I told you when we started this relationship what to expect' by Stephanie Smolensky; 'If I come' by Susan Wallbank; 'Pearly Oats' by Fay Weldon: 1977

'If no revolution come' and 'The Polish husband' by Helen Dunmore; 'Sacrifice' by Eileen Fairweather; 'Dadda' by Marjorie Jackson; 'Shaking Hands with the Middle Ages' by Evelyn Sharp, from *Rebel Women*, published in 1915 by United Suffragists. 'An Unwritten Story: Explanation of (Plus Apology for)' by Nadia Wheatley: 1978

'The Same Day in Westport and Knightsbridge' by Dolly Barrett: 1979

Typeset by Red Lion Setters, Holborn, London

Printed in Great Britain

Contents

Introduction

In the last decade the explosion of women's liberation consciousness across the world has, for the first time, given many thousands of women the conviction that their voices are important. Women have written leaflets, tracts, herstories, position papers, comics and newspapers in a sustained attack on sexist laws, attitudes and institutions, tearing off the veils of the old femininity and saying (or shouting): 'We are not the women you tell us we are; this is who we are and this is what we want to become; this is our experience.'

Since 1972 *Spare Rib* has been a part of this movement of redefinition. The idea of an alternative women's magazine developed out of meetings of women who were angry at the sexism they faced in their work on the underground newspapers of the late 60s and early 70s. When the first issue appeared on British news-stands in July 1972 it was clearly aimed at women unfamiliar with feminist ideas and stood halfway between being a magazine of the counter-culture and a voice of women's liberation. In format and choice of areas to cover, however, *Spare Rib* was similar to any traditional women's magazine, and this was part of a conscious attempt to spread new politics through familiar forms. Fiction, too, appeared as part of that rationale of familiarity — 'and now for this month's story' — although there were attempts at soliciting more participation from readers; an early competition feature, for example, asked readers to finish a story begun in the magazine.

In the first year of *Spare Rib* support from the women's liberation movement for its rather glossy and elegant young sister was neither immediate nor unqualified and a very critical send-up called 'Spare Tit' was circulated at that year's National Women's Liberation Conference. The fiction published in those early days also tended to raise the hackles of a movement which was rather suspicious of individualism, professionalism and 'big name' writers — of which *Spare Rib* published quite a few, including Margaret Drabble, Sylvia Plath, Fay Weldon and Edna O'Brien. By the second year of the magazine, the small initial capital had run out and *Spare Rib*'s workers realised that they could no longer pay writers for stories and articles. At the same time they were beginning to look for work that explored more explicitly feminist territory and since there was very little new feminist writing around, almost no fiction appeared in the magazine that year.

Since then many things have changed. The movement has grown and its ideas have spread. *Spare Rib* has gathered a readership which puts its preferences forcefully — for example, readers expressed disinterest in areas that *Spare Rib* originally tried to cover, like cookery and beauty, and asked for more features which kept them in touch with all the legal, practical and theoretical developments in women's liberation. The format and the issues the magazine dealt with changed in response. *Spare Rib* changed internally too. As it grew more closely connected with the ideas of the women's movement, the organisation of work within the magazine was transformed from a hierarchical structure headed by one editor to a collective in which everyone shares in both editorial and dogsbody tasks. Also the pool of unpaid helpers and supporters of the magazine grew as more and more feminists recognised that *Spare Rib* is a useful way of reaching other women, and began to write, illustrate, photograph and otherwise labour for it.

This period brought a gradual change in the sort of fiction sent to *Spare Rib*. By 1975 the sheaves of traditional magazine stories addressed to 'Dear Sir' had diminished, whereas the clearly feminist work was on the increase as more and more women turned to fictional and poetic forms as a way of exploring their experience and expressing the insights that women's liberation, and consciousness-raising groups, had sparked off. Women were discovering how many ways there were of 'speaking bitterness'. Women writers' collectives were forming too, around that time.

Since there were few outlets for the spiky, political sort of writing that feminist consciousness produced, *Spare Rib* was an obvious place for these women to send their work. Through the magazine they could reach an audience of their peers and get some support for creative writing about *female* experience which might never have seen the light of day if left to the prejudices of the literary establishment. For this kind of fiction was simply too uncomfortable; it turned far too sharp an eye on the way sexism permeates day-to-day life and relationships, particularly sexual relationships, where the analysis was often brutally precise. Merely by addressing itself specifically to women's experience the fiction and poetry in *Spare Rib* explores underdeveloped and undervalued literary territory. This collection reflects that. Much of it digs down into the areas of fiercest struggle and change for women, for example, the hair-tearing pressures of a role as servicer to man-kids-house, which occur time and time again in women's writing, are dissected with black humour in Lynda Schor's 'My Death'. Male-defined sex is seen angrily from the underneath in Rosemary Yates's painful 'Mouselike' and subversively in Tina Reid's ironic 'Eye to Eye'. Taking the long road away from dependence on a husband and towards an independent identity is a theme explored in Ann Oosthuizen's powerful story of widowhood, 'Bones'. The terror and elation of taking direct political action for the first time is described by Evelyn Sharp's suffragette heroine in a story written 60 years ago.

Other themes emerge from the way women are re-examining their childhood and adolescent experience and coming up against the political realities of race and class, as well as sexism. Ros Carne's 'Mrs Mac and the Witch' shows the predicament of a schoolgirl who tries to identify as a lesbian amid enforced heterosexuality; the intensity of the 'best girlfriend' relationship is rediscovered by Stef Pixner in 'O-U-T Spells Out'.

Work outside the home, though a preoccupation of feminist politics, appears rarely as a theme in the British fiction we see at *Spare Rib*. Fay Weldon touches on it in 'Pearly Oats', in which her advertising executive negotiates the terrors of ageing and redundancy, but it is two stories from farther afield — from Sweden and the USSR — which tackle the details of waged work and what it means to a research worker and a production line worker.

When selecting features and fiction at *Spare Rib* we're often struck by how fine the line is between the personal testament or diary-like style many women use to describe their experience in fiction, and the autobiographical true story. The content may be very similar, the form only slightly different — and often the 'true' testaments are as rich in literary and dramatic qualities as the 'fiction'. To illustrate how these categories flow into each other, then, I've cheated slightly and included one 'true' story in the guise of a funny moral fable: 'In the Shit No More', Anya Bostock's tale of a lone woman versus a lavatory seat.

Although we have occasionally solicited particular poems or reprinted poems from American magazines, most *Spare Rib* poetry is chosen from the manuscripts which flood in. Sometimes a poem is used with a particular article; we've done this with articles on subjects ranging from menstruation to women in prison. Astra's 'too late', a poem about her mother, accompanied a feature on homeless women in hostels when it appeared in the magazine. The emphasis in the poetry included here is mainly on the personal voice and on reclaiming female experience: our bodies, our minds, our selves. The search for a self-defined sexuality is the theme of Judith Kazantzis'

'Shout' and Susan Wallbank's 'If I come'. Angela Hamblin's 'Sensitivity' explores the specific vulnerability of pregnancy and Judith Barrington unravels the guilt and pain of the mother-daughter relationship. In the struggle for self-definition, male egotism comes in for a battering: Stephanie Smolensky takes a gleeful revenge on a 'non-sexist' man in her acid poem 'I told you when we started this relationship what to expect'; Natasha Morgan writes wryly of a man who mostly 'feels like a tractor'.

Our approach to selecting work has changed over the last three or four years, as we have dealt with the increasing flow of new writing by feminists. A few years ago we were rather more interested in content than in form; we looked for themes that reflected our experience as feminists and said something about women's position, without worrying too much if the political bones weren't clothed in much artistic flesh. Now we're liable to concern ourselves not just with what's said but also with *how* it's said. This means being involved in searching for the new forms and techniques best fitted to express women's new under-standing. We've also moved towards seeing that a wider range of content — not just that with which we can closely identify — can and should be dealt with. All the time, along with our writers, we are learning and changing.

Of course it isn't possible to select and criticise creative writing for *Spare Rib* without feeling unsure and clumsy, and stumbling from time to time over craggy boulders labelled 'Art' and 'Politics'. Questions about the relationship between these two have inevitably come up because *Spare Rib* fiction and poetry appear in a political magazine. Sometimes our priorities seem unclear. One question which comes up quite often is how far our stories ought to concentrate on an accurate reflection of women's everyday oppression — as in Margaret Rodriguez's 'The Vote', for instance, or Eileen Fairweather's 'Extract from a Novel' — thus risking cries of 'too depressing' from readers. How far should we be trying to publish more stories with 'positive heroines' who will provide new, optimistic role models for women? 'Snow White', as rewritten by the Merseyside Women's Literature Collective, falls unashamedly into the latter bracket and was, in fact, a great favourite. Another more general question concerns what relation feminism has to the act of writing: does its impetus free women to write exactly what they think or does its ideology place its own limitations on the areas they feel they can uncover? These sticky questions can't be transcended but must be worked through in the *doing* of it, in the writing and publishing and reading and discussing.

Then, of course, there are questions raised by writers and critics who are outside feminism but who want to create a fixed category called feminist fiction which can then be written off as inevitably didactic, axe-grinding and humourless. In doing this they fail to see that feminism is not merely a set of campaigns and political strategies; its basis in the idea that the personal is political means that it can and does transform women's consciousness of themselves at a very deep level. And a strong, long-term dose of this changed consciousness and expanded perception of the world is one of the things needed to shock some alertness to life's larger issues back into literature.

But feminist ideas — however deeply they can revolutionise women's view of the world and themselves — aren't above the puritanism and moralism frequently associated with left politics. Feminism needs writers to pit their inquisitive and imaginative wits against the constricting aspects of its ideology — to keep sweeping away at the cobwebs of orthodoxy.

Readers will have to look hard to find simple or dogmatic political messages in these *Spare Rib* stories and poems, which use such a variety of approaches to describe a complex reality. The depth and breadth of the new female consciousness can be judged from the stories collected here, for the anthology gathers together tales of life and how it is lived by women not only in Britain but also in India and Mexico, South Africa and the USSR; stories of girlhood and widowhood, militancy and mothering, war and sex-war. I hope it will engage, stimulate, and inspire others to write — and help pave the way towards a rich and vital contemporary literature which speaks truly to women's experience.

Alison Fell

6

Lynda Schor

My Death

It was cool in the hallway as I locked the carriage to the filthy balustrade. I considered for a moment whether it would be easier to make two trips upstairs with the contents of the stroller and decided to try for one. I didn't like trying to make the decision of whether I preferred my bundles robbed or the baby kidnapped, so I decided to unload everything. With the baby in my arms, I bent down, took out his blanket, bottle and his toys, put them alongside him in one arm, then with the other lifted the huge bag of groceries out by the top of the bag trying to balance it gently so the whole top didn't rip off until I could get it settled in my other arm. The cool, musty air felt good as it dried my perspiration. One more flight, I thought. Then, at the bottom of the second flight of stairs, something happened. I broke out into a cold sweat as I felt the blood leave my head and all my extremities. My heart began beating wildly, tachycardia, in an incredible arhythmia. Then I felt an explosion so large that it was audible too, a sort of light surrounded by blackness which fell down over my eyes leaving a residue of tiny sparks sparkling at the edges, then an incomparable nausea of the whole body, a deep nausea which included even my extremities.

This is it, I thought. What I was always afraid of. Death. I had always thought it would be a stroke, a cerebral accident, as it was called. But maybe that had been a heart attack, or diabetic shock. It most likely was a large blood vessel bursting in the brain, in a sort of explosion, the blood, out of its boundaries in a rush, flooding all over, rushing down over my eyes. That's what my grandmother had died of, and I always knew it would feel like that. It actually felt familiar.

When I didn't feel my heart any more I knew I was dead, but I didn't want to drop the baby, so I thought I'd just try to get upstairs, and too, the thought of all the groceries splattered all along the hall, the ketchup spilled, broken glass, oranges falling down the stairs all the way to the front door; the thought of what the Tenant's Committee would think filled me with dismay. I made a supreme effort, and continued carrying it all upstairs. I rested the groceries against my raised knee as I unlocked the door, fully intending to lie the baby down and then lie down myself, being dead, but as I put the baby down and saw him kicking there on the couch, I felt sudden remorse. I knew I couldn't leave him there because as soon as I actually departed this world he'd probably roll off the couch and cry piteously for hours with no one to hear him. Just as I was trying to figure out what to do with the little guy, he began to cry, and I realised that it was time for him to nurse, and it would be better if I left him fed and comfortable, so I left the food in the bag and lifted my shirt, cradling the baby who felt hot next to my cooling flesh, which must, by now, be way below body temperature, and wondering whether there was still milk in a dead woman's breast. The baby sucked greedily, unaware of my condition. Certain body processes must continue from inertia for a while. I burped him conscientiously, and then he defecated on me right out the edges of his nappie. I decided not to leave him in that condition, and also, I myself didn't want anyone to find me dead with shit on my lap, which brought me to the whole thing of what I should wear. Should I change my

8

underpants? I would have to have my period when I died. Leave it to me to be in the most embarrassing condition. I looked in the mirror and I didn't look good, believe me, but I looked as I imagined I'd look after I saw my grandfather dead, though when I saw him he had more makeup than I; my face was whiter, his was the bluish black of a heart attack. Probably one of the arterioles in my brain had burst. And I had thought that those small lapses into senility I had experienced lately were the result of too much housework. I looked white and solid as if I were made of marble, an article rather than a person. In a lifeless state my face was really ugly, since I wasn't really pretty, the only thing I'd had in my favour was a sort of life, some sex appeal emanating from a type of expressiveness, which, when gone, left my face frightening in its blank sheer ugliness of form.

Just as I'm about to lie down, with great misgivings, as I watch the baby paddle about on the rug, arms and legs moving frantically, but luckily unable to move an inch in either direction except round in a circle, I realise that it's time to pick up the other two kids from school. A person can't even die here, I think, as tears (where can they be welling from?) actually fill my eyes. Maybe I can get someone to pick them up for me. I've already considered calling Dave, but would he leave the store early just because his wife had died? What about when I had the baby and he made me come home two days early from the hospital because he couldn't watch the other two and didn't want to close the store, even for a day. And the time I nearly bled to death from a haemorrhaging extracted wisdom tooth and the dentist wouldn't answer his answering service, and I asked Dave to come home and watch the three kids so I could find an emergency clinic that dispensed dental treatment, and he said he couldn't leave yet because a customer was there. So do you think he'd leave in the middle of the day for a mere death? I decided to call Ruth Roth. Maybe she'd take them to her house, then I wouldn't have to worry about them and Dave could pick them up when he closed his shop.

'Hello, Ruth?'

'Hi'

'Listen, Ruth, I'm dead, could you pick up the kids for me and keep them a while till Dave picks them up?'

'I'm dead too. I was going to call you and ask you whether you could pick up Rosalee.'

'I would, but I'm really dead. I mean dead.'

'I'm worse than dead, I have this virus. Just pick up Rosalee today, I'll do yours tomorrow.' I decided not to hassle. I got ready to pick up my two kids, plus Rosalee.

The proscenium of the school is sickening even when one's feeling well. I suppose it could be uglier aesthetically, but it becomes ugly when one has to go there every day for so many years, stand in the same place, and at a certain moment, mobs of kids begin pouring out, an enormous effusive discharge, a percolating inundating deluge, almost as if the building itself is writhing in the throes of an enormous peristalsis. Every day the same mothers stand there in the same spot and wait. It's depressing. It reminds me of my childhood at Coney Island, standing poor postured in the ocean, skin blotched, burnt and freckled, a mottled child with a slanty buck-toothed grin, always slightly nauseous from the sun, my hair apologetically dripping, waiting in excitement and terror for the next wave.

Timothy and Rosalee, in the same class, are out, running wildly around the stroller, the baby's head swivelling around in complete circles watching them. The two kids, increasingly wild, disturb me. There's no part of me that's sympathetic with the speed of them. I become dizzy and lean on a parked car for support.

'Stop being so wild,' I say, thinking to myself that it's all because Rosalee's here, which is mostly a lie.

'You're going to hurt yourselves,' I say, like an oracle. Their movements accelerate, and interweave with other children, moving in and out, spreading along the whole street, books, noise, and food flying, like a dance choreographed by my worst enemy. And sure enough, Timothy is on the floor, on his chin. As he rises, blood drips in drops to the spot on the concrete where his chin hit, leaving a mark. Everyone crowds around, sympathetic, telling me about all the cases they knew of where a fall on the chinbone required stitches, as I stare at the split flesh hanging at the bottom of my little boy's chin. In a semi-stupor I raise my ass off the royal blue Volkswagen, the fender of which fits more neatly to the body than any other type of car, and rummage around in my huge purse for something to staunch the blood. I find a nappie without too much spit-up on it.

As soon as the wound is covered with the nappie, some of the people, who have become vampires, pull in their teeth and begin moving away again. Timothy is at last quiet as we wait for Alex. Rosalee is also subdued. It would be very pleasant except for the fact that when Alex comes out we'll have to run over to the emergency room at St Vincent's, which, fortunately, is right across the street from the school. Who knows how much foresight went into that seeming coincidence. I see Alex, minus her usual smile.

'What's wrong?' I ask, barely having time to be interested. No answer. This is very common. She's uncommunicative. I quickly consider taking advantage of the situation in order not to have to hear what's the matter.

'What's the matter?'

'ggaaaoo ooooieu mmnn ,,,,,,,, oooiiiffo.' She's said that whole sentence without once opening her mouth, which is excellent except for the fact that I didn't understand a word.

'Timothy fell from being wild with Rosalee,' I tell her, 'and we have to bring him to the clinic. I think he needs stitches.'

'ggooor gigo,' she says with her mouth still closed. What I'd like to do is leave the kids off at David's store before I take Timo to the hospital. It's only about a block and a half out of the way. I peer under the diaper and see that the bleeding seems to have stopped, but I know he'll need stitches by the way it hangs open.

'Let's go,' I say. We all start moving, Timo and Alex each holding one side of the stroller handle, when I notice that Rosalee's not with us. She's standing there fifteen feet behind us

'Come on!' I say, really losing patience. My teeth are clenched. From anger or rigor mortis?

'I can't, my mommy didn't tell me to go with you.'

'Well, she called me up, then it was too late to tell you.'

'She said never to go with anybody.' (I'm just a dead body.)

'I'm Timo's mother.'

'Well, I'm not going.'

'Then you'll be here forever because I'm supposed to pick you up.'

'I don't care, I'll wait here forever for my mommy, and when she sees I'm not with you she'll come and get me.'

'Your ass,' I say, as I pull her as hard as I can and place her hand around the stroller handle with as much pressure as I can, as if I were gluing it there and didn't want it to slip apart.

When we get to David's store, he comes out to meet us, probably in the hope that if he gets to us first he can deflect us from coming into the store and distract us into going home. He's wearing his sneakers, no socks, and a work shirt open to the waist. His brown slender chest, tanned and hairless, is charming, as are his gently hairy ankles emerging from the bottom of his shrunken slacks, and flowing, unbroken by the presence of socks, into his sneakers. He glares.

'I have to leave the kids here to take Timo to the hospital. He fell in front of the school.'

'Why can't you take them. You know they'll be wild here. They might break something.'

'Because I think Timo needs stitches, and the other kids will be disturbing and running around and there's no place to put the stroller, and the baby will breathe infected air. Aside from that, I died this afternoon, I shouldn't even be doing anything. I could lie down right now and no one would be able to call me down for it.'

'You always complain,' he says. I then rip the nappie from where Timo is holding it to his chin, taking advantage of the fact that David can't bear to see any injury, no matter how slight, in order to impress upon him that it's not just for nothing I'm asking him to do this favour. He looks, turns white,

12

puts his arm across his eyes and runs for the store. I park the baby carriage, stuff the pacifier in the baby's mouth, and take off in the opposite direction with Timothy. It takes a few minutes for me to become acclimatised to walking without a stroller in front of me without falling over, but when I do it feels so good that I don't even mind going for stitches. Timo isn't crying. He wants to know whether he can have some candy.

I know where the emergency room is; I've been there before. We wait on a long line to register. I don't know how I manage to remain on my feet. Timothy is holding the nappie to his chin and eating liquorice. It's our turn.

'Name,' says the secretary.

'Timothy Schor.'

'Timothy? That's a strange name for a woman.'

'It's not for me, it's my son.'

'I thought it was you, you look so terrible,' she says.

'Dead people usually look bad,' I say. She looks around in a moment of panic, as if she's trying to spot a psychiatrist on duty. Of course she's unsuccessful. She decides to terminate any communication with me other than the application for treatment. I show her his chin.

'Oh, it's bad, it's like another mouth,' she says coolly.

'Fuck you,' I whisper with my death breath.

'Go to the third room on your left after the large room where the sign is, and wait,' she says. We wait. My fear is that after we wait for four hours or so, we'll find out that they lost the pink paper that the secretary filled out. A nurse comes in.

'Timothy Skor?'

'Yes?' She slips a thermometer under his tongue and times his pulse, as liquorice juice streams out along the sides of the thermometer and dribbles onto the nappie. We wait more. I'm holding his hand. Someone else comes in with a baby. She undresses the baby on a crib. Even though it's summer, the baby has on a sweater and legging ski set and a light woollen bonnet, which has to be removed, then little shoes, underneath, tights, a dress, a tiny slip, a minuscule undershirt. She undresses the baby, leisurely, carefully, right down to one Pamper, weeping gently onto its belly. She folds all the clothes neatly in a pile, takes out a soft baby hairbrush from her large pink carrying case and begins to gently brush its almost nonexistent hair. This must be the grooming instinct, I think. Then I wonder why I lack it, as I look at Timo. His hair is long, it hasn't been combed for a year and a half. He has various food stains on his face which extend down over his shirt in matching and contrasting colours. His face is long, his chin sharp. All of a sudden I feel personally responsible for his injury. Waiting so long makes me angry. I'm considering taking him home and taping his chin together myself. I'm thinking of lying down right here and now so they can say, 'She died waiting for service in the emergency clinic,' but I'm afraid to leave Timo at their mercy.

A doctor comes in. He says, 'Que pasa?'

'He fell,' I say.

'Let's have a look ...... uuuugggggghhhhhh. What happened?' he asks.

'He fell on the concrete in front of the school.'

'What happened, sonny,' he asks Timo.

'I fell on the concrete in front of the school.'

'Are you trying to accuse me of child beating?' I ask.

'Cool it, lady, by the way, this must have upset you, you don't look well. Have a seat.'

'I'm already sitting.'

'Well, relax. I'll tell the nurse to bring you some smelling salts. I'm going to have to take a couple of stitches. You wait here.'

'I want to come with him.'

'I'd rather you didn't, you look so bad, you might faint.'

'If I look bad, it's because I'm dead, smelling salts and waiting here aren't going to help. You think I'm just a hysterical woman,' I screamed, 'But I'm not, I'm simply dead. A person could die waiting here!' I shriek, filling the halls with my mausoleum, creature feature scream.

The doctor runs from the room. A minute later a nurse comes and takes Timo out. The coward is probably waiting, trembling in the sewing room. Where did the doctor learn to sew? In Home Economics? Will they bring back my child? Maybe they'll take me upstairs to the looney section. There's no need to fear that, looney space is at a premium these days. If you really go insane bad you have to wait at Bellevue for an opening here. It's the Concord of mental hospitals. And on the wall, to minimise my sufferings, is a crucifix, a painted metal Christ on a wooden cross, passive, limp, blood, painted with a metallic glow, streaming from every nail wound. Actually he's beyond suffering. As depicted here, he must already be dead. I'm in the process of seeking two cross pieces of wood to fulfil a prank I'm thinking of, and I've already shredded my clothes and painted red on me, when they bring in Timo, with shiny dried tear rivulets and a stretched mouth.

'Make an appointment to bring him to the sewing clinic next week to have the stitches removed,' he says.

At the cashier I say, 'How much is it?'

'Sixteen dollars for a visit to the emergency room, plus four stitches at ten dollars a stitch, that's forty, plus sixteen, plus the X-rays that they took to see whether the bone was chipped, and the entire body X-rays they took to see whether he showed signs of previous child-battering.'

'You expect me to pay for the unauthorised X-rays that you took for your own use, having nothing to do with my child's injury??????! You get a special grant for that! I should sue you for exposing him to unnecessary X-rays!'

'Lady, I didn't take the X-rays, so don't say "you". I'm only the cashier.'

'Just send me a bill, I don't carry that much money, even Rockerfeller doesn't. He has credit cards. Do you accept credit? How about Bank Americard?' She hides under the desk as we walk away.

'Where were you so long?' asks Dave, when we return. Does he think we lied to him in order to go see a movie or something?

'How much did it cost?' he asks.

'I'm not sure, they want to charge for X-rays I didn't tell them to do.'

'Well, you have to pay out of the household money, since it was all due to your neglect.' I hold Timothy to me and weep into his bandage.

'Don't get it wet,' he says.

On the way home the baby begins to cry. I buy some milk, not knowing when a dead woman's milk gives out. I recall photos I've seen of dead Indian women (starvation) with emaciated babies at the breast, but I never could tell whether they were still sucking. Or if they were, were they getting anything. At home, baby at my breast, I see I was wise to buy the milk. I make a bottle. The best way to wean someone from you is to die. Who said that? Was it Eleanor Roosevelt? Edmund Muskie? Flo Kennedy, probably, or Ethel. Alex still looks unhappy. I ask her what's the matter. She gives me a pathetic look and bares her teeth. There's nothing there. She has no front teeth anymore. And it isn't as if they've just fallen out, on the contrary, new large ones had just grown in, just achieved their full growth within the past week or so. And since they had been enormous, it wasn't easy to miss them.

'What happened?' I say. I don't yell. Her face turns into a prune and tears run like streams in and out of the creases and into her mouth.

'Why are you crying?'

'Because I thought you were going to yell.' Well to tell you the truth, I felt like yelling, I felt like screaming, but it's really stupid to yell at a kid because her teeth are knocked out. And they weren't completely knocked out, just chipped off almost to the top. A good dentist could cap them.

Actually I had thought that when David finally came home he'd take over so that I could just die normally. It isn't so much that I wanted to die, but being already dead, there was no choice, there was something compelling about lying down. I did have dinner ready for him so that things wouldn't be too much of a strain. I also prepared food for the next four days, cold things, and wrapped them and labelled them with instructions for warming or serving. When he came in he looked at me for a minute and said, 'you don't look well.' I said, 'Well, it's because I'm dead, and usually dead people aren't well.'

'Don't be so sarcastic,' he said. 'You always complain. Think of something more positive, for instance, at least you can't get cancer now. Why don't you make some coffee to take your mind off it?'

'Look,' I said, 'I'm dead and I'm going to lie down. Make yourself some instant coffee.'

'Instant coffee is horrible.'

'Them make yourself some regular.'

'But you know I can't make it as good as you, I don't know how much coffee to put in.' I made the coffee, trying to figure out where to lie down when I finally could. The whole thing seemed so unnatural at this point. It's best to just lie down at the moment you die, no matter where it is. Did that mean I should descend the hall stairs and collapse at the point where I originally died? The kids were watching Gilligan's Island and the baby was sleeping. I lay down on the bed and a gentle peace pervaded me, which was shattered by David, calling — 'Hey, where's my dinner?' He called again. I wondered whether I was capable of ever getting up again. I ignored him. Eventually he'd see something was wrong and that I'd never be able to make his dinner again, or else he'd get his own dinner. He continued calling an endless number of times. Finally he came in and throttled me.

'What's wrong?' he said.

'I told you. I'm dead.'

'You're just a hypochondriac. Move over.' He lay down beside me, squeezed in, because I didn't move over. Then he moved on top of me.

'How can you do this to a dead person?' I was really indignant over the indignity.

'Well, I'll try, it's sort of exciting.' He disembarked for one mad moment while he ripped off his clothes. Then he proceeded to rip off mine, which was difficult since I didn't even raise my hips.

'Why can't you move just a little?' he said. 'I feel like a

necrophiliac.'

'Why does your excitement depend on mine? You're insecure. You take it too personally. It's a known fact that dead
people don't respond.'

I put the kids to bed. I looked in the mirror. My face was
already thinner, my eyes looked like melted fish eyes. My skin
was like cheesecake with birthday candle blue lips. I felt like
weeping but not a tear came to my concave fish eye.

I sat on the toilet while I let my bathwater in, nice and hot. I
left my hand under the tap where it flipped to and fro like a
seal flipper. When the tub was full I got into the water gently,
insinuating my body in a bit at a time, enjoying the sensual
pleasure of the extreme heat of the lower part of my body and
the gooseflesh of the upper, unimmersed portions. When the
sensation mitigated I rested my back against the curved back of
the tub and slowly lowered my body down. I continued sliding
down until I felt the water crawling over my lips, feeling the
water in my nose, over my eyes and tickling my scalp as it flooded
fluidly through my hair. I never bothered coming up. I noticed
that the oblivion I was experiencing was no different from the
usual.

Ros Carne

Mrs Mac and the Witch

The low droning of the organ voluntary reverbera-
ted through the old stone building, drawing to a close as Mr
Wilshire the vicar stepped up to the dais. It was cool inside the
church and some of the children wore Sunday sweaters, woolly
green V-necks over grey and white checked cotton; they were
squeezed along the front two rows, flanked at each end by a
member of staff. Behind them, empty lines, and then the
village people, not many, now stiffly seated or bent to pray.
Sarah looked down from the choir stalls to her schoolmates in
the nave, all fidgets and bubble gum. They appeared to enjoy
themselves, and she was feeling a bit itchy and hot in the thick,
black, tight-fitting cassock, but she had no regrets over the
promotion.

Her eyes shifted, focusing on the dark female figure in the
organ box, Mrs MacIllvennie in her dusty brown cardigan, the
heavy weight of hair pinned up on top of her head. She had her
back to Sarah who stood looking at the plump white arm
stretching down sideways to the music pile, and then the
profiled cheek of the long sad face. 'Like a horse,' said Angela

Peters, house prefect. 'Do you think so?' queried Sarah, shyly, fixing mentally on that long-limbed and graceful beast. The mass of hair looked heavier than ever today. Sarah could see it loose. Heavy yes, but wild too and windblown like in those pictures in the Wagner book her mother had given her.

They were praying now, heads and trunks sunk down behind the wooden rails. Two more prayers, two more hymns, that would be about twenty minutes, then the anthem. One of the senior girls would take over on the organ and the congregation would sit, while the choir warbled out the Latin words, responding to the lively flourishes of Mrs MacIllvennie's baton. You could feel quite special up there singing your own song. Choir was certainly a lot better than wasting time blowing bubbles with all those sillies in the nave. If you wanted to join you had to audition. All alone in Mrs MacIllvennie's flat. Rehearsals every Tuesday evening. Soon they'd be more frequent because of the concert. Angela Peters said that if you got a solo part you had to go for special practices on your own nearly every day. 'Awful bore,' she told Sarah, 'I did it last year to get out of Mamselle's embroidery class. But it wasn't worth it. Up in that smelly old flat, hanging around for ages while Mrs Mac finishes the washing up and puts her snotty kid to bed ... urgh ... ' Mrs Mac washing up, putting Maisie to bed. There was something so shamefully intimate in the scene that Sarah flushed. She wondered if Mrs Mac still wore her hair in a bun at home. And did she always look so unhappy? Even there? She could never think of Mrs Mac without a vague and cloudy concern. Though sometimes it seemed as if she herself would be the one to suffer in the faint anxiety that emanated from the long pale face.

'The congregation will now stand for hymn number 268, "All ye mountains and streams, praise ye the Lord".' Shuffling feet, people rising slowly as the organ played the introductory bars. And now there seemed to be a scuffle in the front row. Miss Jones was leaning over, making signs, mouthing reprimand. She had edged along in front of the singers, moving in between Patsy Dawson and one of the boys. It was Russ Halter, ginger haired, freckled, confident and noisy. He must have been having a go at Patsy, she was always pushed into the end seat. Sarah felt that sense of disturbance, that mixture of pity and disgust which so often came over her when she thought of the other girl. Disgust yes, but mingled strangely with that same not entirely selfless concern she felt for Mrs Mac. But Sarah could only rationalise part of the way, for didn't each call out her sympathy? She was not alone in feeling sorry for Patsy, all the girls did. Though she did have that funny voice and you really had to stop yourself laughing when she started to talk. The boys called her Dawson the Witch. Well, they were horrid. Though she did look a bit witchy with her straggly black hair twisted into two stringy plaits. Sarah wasn't going to call her 'witch' ... but she was certainly glad Patsy wasn't in the choir. It didn't matter about the others. She never really noticed or bothered about them. But somehow Patsy would have upset the link, for link there was, Sarah was sure, between her and the headmaster's wife. Sometimes in daydreams she would tell her and Mrs Mac would touch her arm, smile. Sarah never knew exactly what came next, and, anyway, there wasn't anything definite, just a blurred sense of the long, horse-like face with the heavy black hair ... Maisie ... the washing up ... and running over ye mountains and streams like the women in the Wagner book. Perhaps Sarah would write her a letter? But no, there was something dull, something much too definite about a letter. What they both felt, she and Mrs Mac, was something finer, something more elevated than could be expressed in mere prose. No, Sarah, who had just discovered John Keats, knew what she would do, she would write her a poem.

Russ Halter was standing on the table at the front of the classroom waving a piece of paper. There was shouting, uproar, people bobbing up and down on the desks, feet stomping on the chalky floor. With ten minutes to go before the third period the room was already crowded out.

'Everybody shut up and I'll read it,' shouted Russ, his face creased in merriment.

'Go on then,' said plump bouncing Delia who stood closest him. And, appealing to the crowd she added loudly, 'Serve her right, dirty lezzie,' dwelling with a sensual relish on the long hard sibilants.

Her arm was stretched out over their heads and pointed to the thin pale faced girl by the back wall. The noise, after the lull, was once again deafening, as Sarah, standing by the wall and following the sign, stared intently at the alien creature with the straggly black hair twisted into two stringy plaits. Stunned and upright in her chair, Patsy's dull eyes were fixed on the boy with the paper. Sarah's stomach seemed to churn. If Patsy was really a witch? And what was a 'lezzie'? She didn't dare ask.

Delia had climbed on the table where she stood close by Russ. Waving and shouting together, self-appointed leaders, they tried to silence the mob.

'Lezzie, lezzie, Patsy's a lezzie.' Other sounds were fading as the classroom started to join in. At first hesitant they swelled to battle pitch as their confidence increased and just as a slow rhythmic hand-clap rises among an impatient audience so their loudly spasmodic occasional cries grew to a reiterated and relentless chanting ... 'LES ... BI ... LES ... BI ... LES ... BI ... LES ... BI ... AN ... LESBIAN.' Sarah stood silent. She gripped the table's edge hard and her knuckles whitened as she continued to stare at Patsy. The girl's expression was changing. What had been a blankness, almost a vacancy, was tensing, hardening into an angularity of pain and hatred. In a moment she would act. As if in that expectancy the chanting had begun to fade and with it the wall of defensively massed bodies that had grown up with the resounding phrases. Some flopped onto desks, others moved to nearby chairs. But the twenty pairs of eyes like twenty loaded rifles were still trained on the trembling girl. She drew herself up from the chair, afraid but hostile and as latently fierce as a cornered rat. For a moment there was silence, broken as she backed slowly around the edge of the wall to the door, her heavy lace-ups clattering on the thin raised floor. People slid away as she approached, whether out of pity or fear it was hard to say for the myth of the witch was strong.

Suddenly a voice cried out, 'Urgh, she touched me.'

The room would have rushed on Patsy and she knew it; lips parted and teeth clenched, she faced them sharply with narrow eyes. Silence again, then sudden sound as she crashed open the classroom door, stumbling wildly out down the steps and off across the grass.

'If I incline unto wickedness with mine heart ...' The psalm, set to music by Mrs Barbara MacIllvennie had an unlikely lilting tune. She stood now, centred on the dais, directing the choir with raised and flickering eyebrows, precise and delicate baton movements. Her faint smile broadened with the successful final cadence and the choir sat down as tubby little Willy Wilshire stood to give the sermon. 'Pray without ceasing' came the words from the top of his nose. It might promise badly but it was certainly easy enough to read comics or play jacks behind the high wooden frontage of the choir stalls. Sarah pulled a crumpled magazine from the sleeve of her cassock and started to flip through. *True Romance*. It was one of those Delia Craddock had lent her, for she had laughed at Sarah's animal stories and the poetry she liked to read. And now, flipping through, pretending nonchalance, she was sharply aware of Delia's peach scented presence close to her on the bench.

Throughout the anthem, watching the white mask of the headmaster's wife behind those lively rhythmic gestures, Sarah had felt herself exposed by sound. It was as if each sung word were a proclamation of her most intimate thoughts. And however confused those thoughts, however undefined those emotions, Sarah knew they were something she could never share with Delia. It was as though the incident in the classroom had cracked her delicate eggshell of protection. Sarah may have been 'toffee-nose' to her schoolmates, but the charge had never been completely serious, and she had always had a comforting sense that despite or perhaps because of a sustained emotional distance she had been widely if not universally admired. But now everything appeared to be whirled about in reverse. It began to seem crucially important not only that she should be liked by Delia but that she herself should be like her.

Still musing over *True Romance* she picked up a whisper in her ear.

'Are you coming to the den tonight?'

'Dunno. I'll tell you later. OK?' Delia nodded.

The den was a small store room at the lower end of the attic. It was packed tight with trunks, two of which had been arrayed with rugs to form make-shift couches. (Sarah knew because she had sneaked in alone one day when no one was around.) Delia often went in there with Russ where they 'did it ... as far as number six'. Tonight there was to be a party. Russ would bring his radio, some of the other boys might come too, and there'd be cards and coca-cola and potato crisps. 'That's all,' Delia had added, as if to reassure the other girl. But Sarah wasn't very sure. The den and all it signified had to date played very little part in her consciousness. Even now there seemed to be little room in her troubled soul for any clear consideration of the connotations of 'an evening in the den'. Still leafing through *True Romance* she glanced down the nave.

The school seemed unusually quiet. Russ, never still, was fidgeting a bit, winking and making signs towards Delia in the choir, but other faces appeared glum, almost vacuous. And there was one less body in the second row. Patsy Dawson wasn't there. She hadn't been seen for a fortnight. When asked, Matron had simply said, 'She's gone home for a while, to be quiet. She's not a well child you know.' But if she hadn't been well why couldn't she have stayed in the san? Others did. Matron could give no answer. 'I really can't say Sarah. Hadn't you best forget about it. She was never a close friend of yours if I remember rightly.' ' ... Never a close friend ... ' Was Matron being purposely cruel? Sarah blenched slightly. She knew only too well why the girl had left. Patsy was not sick, at least not physically. But she had been in pain, fearful pain, while those who had inflicted the pain kept silent, Sarah too, who felt her responsibility to be as great, possibly greater than any of the others'. She had thought about Patsy a lot in those two weeks, more than she thought about Russ or Delia, almost more than she thought of Mrs Mac who sat ahead of her now in the organ box, a heavy weight of hair piled high on top of her head. Sarah was trying not to look at her and, just as she had tried not to think of Patsy, was trying not to think of her. Then the strong sweet smell of body talc hit her senses ... Delia, leaning towards her ...

'Have you decided? I don't know why you're so worried. Nobody's going to do anything to you.'

'It's not that.' In her mind she could see Russ Halter, his grinning freckled face creased in merriment. And she saw Patsy tear stained and dragging her awkward feet across the floor. And then the image seemed to become blurred, melting into that of a much older woman with long black hair and a look of strained sadness in her eyes. And with the image came the smell of dishwater, mingled with baby lotion, in the woman's home where she washed up dishes and fed her dribbling, snotty-nosed child. To Sarah it seemed as if the firm ground she had walked on all her life were somehow giving way. She was sinking, slowly, and soon might fall. And there in front of her was an island, and on that island stood Delia, and Russ, shouting, waving, just as they had done in the classroom. But they were smiling too.

'Come up and join us,' they were saying. 'It's easy, we're safe here. Come on, just climb up.' The voices became louder, more insistent, until she realised Delia beside her was shaking her arm.

'What's up? Are you asleep? Look. I was going to show you the poem. Did you ever see it?' And she drew a tattered fold of paper from the pocket of her blouse. It seemed familiar, not because Sarah had remembered, but because it seemed she knew quite instinctively what it would be. She took it, slowly. Unfolding that scrap of dog-eared file paper it was as if she had already read the words many times over and all the time she was sinking, sinking. The very shape of the letters was already engraved inside her head, the thirteen lines of well scanned verse above which were printed in a script painstakingly neat the words 'To Barbara', and then in brackets '(Mrs MacIllvennie)'.

She had sunk deep now. The ground above appeared to be closing over the space of light. But there was still the island, and an arm which seemed to reach into the pit to save her. The arm was Delia's. Sarah spoke.

'Did you say seven o'clock? OK. I'll come. I'm sorry it's taken me so long to decide ... I suppose I don't want the boys to think I'll just come running whenever they call.' And she looked up at Delia who smiled and pulled her ashore.

A traditional tale as retold by

The Merseyside Women's Literature Collective

Snow White

High above a far off kingdom, carved into the rock of a mountainside, there once stood a mighty castle. It was so high that the people working on the distant plain could look up and see it among the clouds and when they saw it they trembled, for it was the castle of the cruel and powerful Queen of the Mountains.

The Queen of the Mountains had ten thousand soldiers at her command. She sat upon a throne of marble dressed in robes weighed down with glittering jewels, and holding in her hand a magic mirror. This mirror could answer any question the Queen asked it and in it the Queen could see what was happening anywhere in her kingdom. When she looked into the mirror and saw any of her subjects doing things which displeased her she sent soldiers to punish them.

Night and day her soldiers stood guard on the walls of the castle and every day they watched as people from all over the kingdom toiled up the steep pathway carrying heavy loads: iron to shoe the royal horses; weapons to arm the royal soldiers; food to be cooked in the royal kitchens; cloth to clothe the royal servants. The procession wound on and on up the mountain-side to the castle. The people were carrying with them all the useful and beautiful things that had been made in the kingdom, for everything they made belonged to the Queen and they were allowed to keep only what was left over or spoiled.

No one could save anything from the Queen of the Mountains for no place was hidden from her magic mirror. Every day the riches of the kingdom were brought to her and every night she asked the mirror:

> 'Mirror, mirror in my hand,
> Who is happiest in the land?'

Then in a silvery voice the mirror always replied:

> 'Queen, all bow to your command,
> You are the happiest in the land.'

And the Queen would smile.

One day, among the procession climbing the steep path to the castle were a pale little girl called Snow White and seven little men, dwarfs, even smaller than her. Snow White and the dwarfs were carrying between them a heavy chest bound with metal bands. They had travelled all the way from the diamond mines beside the distant sea. There, far underground, often in danger, they and many other men, women and children worked long and weary hours. Every year they must send a chestful of diamonds to the Queen of the Mountains or they would be cruelly punished.

When the other people in the procession reached the castle gates the lovely things they had been carrying were taken from them and they were sent away, but Snow White and the seven dwarfs were surrounded by soldiers and brought to the throne room of the Queen herself.

'Open the chest,' ordered the Queen as they bowed low before her.

Two dwarfs lifted the lid. The chest was full of glittering

28

diamonds and on top of them lay a necklace shaped like branches of ice. The Queen held the necklace up to the light.

'Did you make this?' she asked Snow White.

'Yes Majesty,' said the girl.

'It is well made,' said the Queen. 'You are to stay in the castle as a jewellery maker.'

Snow White's pale cheeks turned red and she opened her mouth to cry 'No!' but each of the seven dwarfs put a crooked finger to his lips, warning her to be silent.

'Take her to the workshop!' ordered the Queen.

The soldiers led Snow White and the dwarfs out of the throne room and up a twisting stairway to a small room at the top of a tower. In the room there was a work bench with jeweller's tools laid out on it. All around the walls, stored in tall glass jars, gleamed jewels of many colours: amethysts, emeralds, rubies, sapphires, topaz. Little light came through the one small window but the jewels shone so brightly that when Snow White looked at them her eyes were dazzled and her head began to ache.

Snow White and the dwarfs took the diamonds from the chest and put them into empty glass jars. Then, one by one, the seven little men kissed Snow White goodbye. There were tears in their eyes for she was their dearest friend. They shouldered the empty chest and went slowly down the twisting staircase.

'You are very lucky,' said one of the soldiers to Snow White. 'You will no longer be poor and lead a hard life toiling underground in the mine. Here servants will wait on you. You will sleep in a soft, scented bed and be brought whatever delicious food and drink you want. And, if the Queen is especially pleased with your work she will give you rich rewards.'

'But my friends will still be toiling in the mine,' said Snow White and her heart felt like a stone with sorrow.

In the long days and weeks which followed Snow White grew more and more skilful at making beautiful pieces of jewellery out of the precious stones and metals in the workshop. The jewellery pleased the Queen of the Mountains. One evening she summoned Snow White to the throne room.

'This brooch pleases me,' said the Queen. 'You may choose a reward.'

'Oh, Majesty,' answered Snow White, falling on her knees, 'please let me go home.'

The Queen was angry. She turned her mirror towards Snow White and in it the little girl could see the dwarfs and all her other friends digging in the mine and dragging heavy loads along its narrow tunnels.

'You could have anything your heart desires and yet you ask to return to that miserable life!' the Queen exclaimed. 'Go back to your work and think hard before you enter my presence again.'

So, as she deftly twisted the metal and fitted the precious stones, Snow White thought long and hard. She thought of the sufferings she had shared with her friends in the distant mines; of how they and all the people of the land spent their whole lives working to make lovely things for the Queen of the Mountains while they themselves had barely enough to live on. And Snow White knew what she would ask for.

'I will make a jewelled belt so beautiful that the Queen will call me before her again,' she thought and at once set to work.

'Well, Snow White,' said the Queen as the girl stood before her throne a second time, 'you have had time to think. Tell me your heart's desire and I will grant it, for what you have made is more beautiful than anything in my treasure chambers.' As she spoke the Queen ran her fingers along the red and purple gems of the jewelled belt.

'Majesty,' said Snow White, 'I have thought and what I ask for is this: take only what you need from the people of the kingdom and let them keep the rest so that they will no longer be cold and hungry and miserable.'

The Queen's eyes glittered with rage and her hand tightened on the jewelled belt, but when she spoke her voice was as sweet as honey.

'Snow White, if anyone but you had spoken such treachery, I would have ordered my soldiers to throw them from the walls of the castle onto the rocks below. But you have a rare skill and are young enough to change your thoughts. Come close and look in my mirror.'

Snow White looked into the magic mirror and saw herself reflected there, but strangely. She was wearing working clothes and yet in the mirror she was dressed in a richly embroidered gown, pearls and rubies were entwined in her long hair and on her head was a golden crown.

'You see, Snow White,' said the Queen, 'you could be a princess. Now go.'

Snow White went back to the workshop. She stood gazing out of the tiny window and thinking of how she had looked in the mirror, adorned with jewels and gold. Far below her she could see the daily procession of people carrying up the mountainside all the things they had made and must give to the Queen. Beyond them the green plain stretched out until it reached the distant hills. On the other side of the hills was the sea and Snow White's home. The words of a song which she and her friends used to sing when the long day's work in the mine was over came back to her mind.

> *Emerald's green but grass is greener*
> *Sapphires pale beside the sea.*
> *No jet as black as the wild night sky,*
> *No ruby red*
> *No ruby red*
> *No ruby red as hearts which cry to be free.*

'What my friends long for is my heart's desire too,' thought Snow White, 'but the Queen of the Mountains will never set us free.'

Soon the Queen summoned Snow White before her throne a third time.

'No flower in all my gardens is as delicately shaped as these earrings you have made,' she said. 'What reward do you want?'

'Nothing, Majesty,' said Snow White quietly.

'Foolish girl!' cried the Queen, 'I know you are unhappy, yet you only have to ask and you can become a princess. Very well, you will continue to make jewellery for me, but from now on soldiers will stand guard at the foot of the tower where you work and unless you choose to be a princess you will never leave the tower again.'

The months passed by. Still Snow White remained alone in the tower and did not ask for her reward. Quiet and pale, she sat at her work, thinking and waiting.

When a whole year had passed Snow White looked from her tiny window and saw below, among the people toiling up the pathway to the castle, seven little figures carrying between them a heavy chest. It was her friends the dwarfs at last.

Snow White waited for the dwarfs to bring the chest of diamonds to the workshop but when the chest was brought in it was carried by some of the Queen's soldiers.

'The Queen has given orders that you are not to see your friends from the mine,' said one of the soldiers. 'She is watching them in her mirror all the time they are here.'

'Please go back to the foot of the stairs and leave me alone,' said Snow White in a sad voice. 'I will fill the glass jars with diamonds and put the empty chest outside the door.'

The soldiers did as she asked, for they liked Snow White and secretly admired her for daring to displease the Queen.

An hour later they returned and took the chest away, down the twisting stairway and into the courtyard where the dwarfs were waiting. The little men swung it on to their shoulders and carried it out of the castle gates and down the mountainside.

All that day the Queen of the Mountains sat on her throne and watched in her mirror as the dwarfs went farther and farther away. By the time that evening came they had crossed the distant hills. The Queen smiled to herself and asked the mirror her usual question:

> *Mirror, mirror in my hand*
> *Who is happiest in the land?'*

In its silvery voice, the mirror replied:

> *'Though all bow to your command,*
> *Snow White is happiest in the land.'*

'Snow White!' hissed the Queen, 'Show me Snow White!'

Then, in the mirror, she saw the seven dwarfs lifting the lid off the chest and out of the chest climbed Snow White, her face full of joy.

The Queen's rage was terrible. She ordered that the soldiers who had let Snow White escape were to be thrown from the castle walls. Throughout the night she sat on her throne speaking to no one. Then, as the sun rose, she gave orders to her soldiers.

'Go to the diamond mines,' she commanded. 'Seal up the entrance while Snow White and her companions are working so that they will all die underground.'

Many of the soldiers were filled with horror but they dared not disobey. The Queen watched in her mirror as they sealed up the way out of the mine and when it was done, she laughed.

Word of the terrible thing done at the Queen's command spread quickly through the land. Many people came to where the Queen's soldiers stood guard beside the sealed up entrance to the mine. As the day wore on, more and more people arrived. They stood there quietly at a little distance from the soldiers, as if they were waiting for something to happen. By evening, a great crowd had gathered. They lit fires to keep themselves warm through the night and talked in low voices about all the people trapped underground and about the cruelty of the Queen of the Mountains. They knew that by now there must be very little air left to breathe down the mine. Soon Snow White and her friends would be dead as the Queen of the Mountains had commanded.

Suddenly, among some rocks on the outskirts of the crowd, a tapping sound could be heard. As the people looked at each other in bewilderment, one of the rocks began to move and then was pushed aside from behind to reveal a narrow shaft going deep into the earth. Climbing from this passage was one of the dwarfs.

'Just in time,' wheezed the dwarf. 'I do not think we could have gone on digging much longer. My oldest brother remembered that when he was very young there was another way out of the mine. He led us to the place and we dug in the dark until the way was opened up.'

One by one, helping each other, the workers from the diamond mine climbed out into the fresh night air. Some were faint, some were bruised and many had torn and bleeding hands, but every child, woman and man was safe. Among them was Snow White.

The great crowd of people round the fires and the soldiers stared in amazement. Then the people began to cheer. Some of the soldiers joined in the cheering but others drew their weapons. One of these called out to Snow White.

'Snow White,' he ordered, 'you must come with us at once back to the castle.'

'No,' answered Snow White, 'I will not go back to the castle and we will send no more diamonds to the Queen. Everyone will keep the things they make and send nothing to the Queen of the Mountains.'

As she spoke the cheers grew louder and louder.

'Then we will kill you,' said the soldier.

'You may kill some of us,' said Snow White, 'but in the end you will lose for there are far more people than there are soldiers.'

The people realised that this was true and they surrounded the soldiers determined to take their weapons from them, whatever the cost.

Far away on her marble throne, the Queen of the Mountains took the jewellery Snow White had made and broke it into pieces. In her magic mirror she could see all that was happening. She knew that the people of the land were rising up against her.

> *'Mirror, mirror in my hand*
> *Make them bow to my command,'*

she ordered her mirror. But the mirror answered:

> *'Queen who was so rich and grand*
> *The people cast you from their land.'*

The magic mirror misted over and when the mist had gone, the Queen could see nothing reflected there but her own face.

Still grasping the mirror in her hand, the Queen of the Mountains rose from her throne and climbed the stone steps to the highest battlements of the castle. From there she could look out and see with her own eyes the crowds of people gathering on the distant plain. In fear and fury she lifted the mirror above her head and flung it from the castle wall.

The mirror would not leave her hand. She fell with it and hurtled screaming down and down until she was shattered into fragments on the rocks below.

Evelyn Sharp

Shaking Hands with the Middle Ages

> *Evelyn Sharp was already a published novelist when she came across the Women's Social and Political Union in 1906. Her feminist beliefs quickly led her into public speaking which terrified her, 'though open warfare is always preferable to the frozen hostility of the drawing-room crowd', and she took part in paper-selling and heckling at Liberal meetings, activities which exposed her to violence and harassment, and which inspired this story. In 1911 she became assistant editor of* Votes for Women *and continued with suffrage militancy through the war years until 1918 when, with the Pethwick-Lawrences, she helped draw up the Reform Bill which finally granted women the vote.*
>
> *'Shaking Hands with the Middle Ages' comes from the collection* Rebel Women, *published in 1915.*

'Going to be a good meeting, don't you think?' chatted one of the men wearing a steward's button to a woman dressed in black, who sat in the front row of the little block of seats reserved for ladies, just below the platform.

She gave an indifferent glance round the hall.

'Yes,' she acquiesced; 'I suppose it is. I've never been to a political meeting before.'

'Really?' said the steward blandly. 'Quite an experience for you, then, with a Cabinet Minister coming!'

He hurried away, unaware of the touch of condescension that had jarred indescribably, and spoke in an eager undertone to a large stout gentleman who was inspecting tickets at the ladies' entrance.

'It's all right,' he said officiously. 'I've just been talking to her. She isn't one of them.'

The stout gentleman looked over his shoulder. 'Who? That one next my wife? Oh, no! She's not their sort. Besides, they all wear green or purple, or both. I'm up to their dodges by this time — just had to turn away quite a nice little girl in a green hat —'

'My sister!' observed the other. 'Oh, it don't matter; I let her in by the side door, and it won't do her any harm. They've got so out of hand, some of these canvassers, since the general election.'

The large steward observed with an indulgent smile that one must make allowances. He did not say for what or for whom, but his meaning seemed to be clear to the other steward.

'The eternal feminine, eh?' he remarked with a knowing nod; and all the men standing round laughed immoderately. Under cover of this exhibition of humour, a girl in grey, with a fur cap and muff, was allowed to pass in without any special scrutiny. She moved very deliberately along the front chairs, which were not filled, stood for an instant facing the audience while she selected her seat, then made her way to one in the middle of a row.

'Votes for women!' piped a wit in the gallery, reproducing the popular impression of the feminine voice; and the audience, strung up to the point of snatching at any outlet for emotion, rocked with mirth.

The girl in grey joined in the laughter. 'Every one seems very jumpy tonight,' she observed to her neighbour, a lady in tight black satin who wore the badge of some Women's Federation. 'I was actually taken for a Suffragette in the market-place just now.'

'Were you, now?' returned the lady, sociably. 'No wonder they're a trifle apprehensive after the way those dreadful creatures went on at the Corn Exchange last week. You were there, perhaps?'

The girl in grey said she was there, and the Federation woman proceeded to converse genially. 'Thought I'd seen your face somewhere,' she said. 'A splendid gathering, that would have been a glorious triumph for the Party, if it hadn't been for those —' She paused for a word, and found it with satisfaction — 'females. Females,' she repeated distinctly. 'You really can't call them anything else.'

'I suppose you can't,' said the girl demurely. The sparkle lit up her eyes again. 'Our minister called them bipeds, in the pulpit, last Sunday,' she added.

'And so they are!' cried the lady in tight black satin. 'So they are.'

'They are,' agreed the girl in grey.

In the front row of chairs, speculation was rife as to the possible presence of Suffragettes. The wife of the man at the door, a homely little woman with a pleasant face, was assuring everybody who cared to know that the thing was impossible.

'They've drafted five hundred police into the town, I'm told; and my husband arranged for thirty extra stewards at the last minute, because the detectives wired that two of them had travelled down in the London train,' she informed a circle of interested listeners.

'Is that why there are so many men wearing little buttons?' asked the woman on her left. 'I wondered if that was usual at political meetings.'

'I think I heard you say you'd never been to a meeting before, didn't I?' said her neighbour pleasantly. 'Neither have I, and I wouldn't be wasting my time here tonight if it wasn't to please my husband. He likes to see women take an interest in politics; it was him that got our member a hundred and twenty-eight canvassers, last election. Oh, he thinks a lot of women, does my husband; says he hasn't any objection to their having a vote, either, only they ought to be ashamed of themselves for going on so about it. I don't hold with votes myself. It's only men that's got all that idle time on their hands, and if they're respectable married men, there's nothing else to occupy them but politics. But for a woman it's work, work, work, from wedding-day till her funeral, and how can she find time for such nonsense? "You've got to be made to think, Martha," he says to me, coming here tonight. Think? If a woman stops to think, she don't stop with her husband, chances are. Of course, he don't believe me when I say that. He's too sure of me, that's where it is.'

'That is always where it is,' said the woman in black, quietly.

Her neighbour took out some knitting. 'They laugh at me for bringing my knitting everywhere,' she said. 'I can't listen if I sit idle. Not that I want to listen,' she concluded, as she settled down comfortably to the counting of stitches.

The organ boomed out a jerky tune with elephantine lightness, and the audience vented its impatience in a lusty rendering of some song about England and liberty. The music was uninspiring, the words were clap-trap, and seemed to convey the singular idea that freedom had been invented and patented within recent years by a particular political party; but the indifferent expression of the woman in black changed and softened as the chorus rose and fell, and a tall man with a lean, humorous face, who stood looking at her, gave her a smile of understanding as the echoing sounds died away. He too was wearing a steward's button, she noticed.

'There's a sort of barbaric splendour about that, isn't there?' he remarked.

She felt none of the irritation that had been roused by the conversational advances of the other steward. It was a relief, indeed, to talk about something ordinary with a man who, she felt instinctively, knew how to give even ordinary things their true values.

'It's the whole effect,' she answered impulsively. 'The

cathedral outside, and this thirteenth-century interior, and then — this!' She looked round the magnificent old County Hall, and along the densely packed rows of restless modern men and women, and then back again, half whimsically, at the man who had spoken to her. 'It is like reaching back to shake hands with the Middle Ages,' she said.

'To fight with the Middle Ages,' he amended, and they both laughed. 'You will find,' he added narrowing his eyes a little to look at her, 'that the Middle Ages generally win, when we hold political meetings here in the provinces.'

There was a distant sound of cheering, and everyone stiffened into attention. A stir ran round the hall; doors were closed with a good deal of noise, and the stewards, looking apprehensively at the little block of seats in the front, gradually closed round them until the gangways were entirely blocked at that end of the hall. One lady, who complained that she could not see the platform for stewards, instantly found herself placed under observation, and was only freed from suspicion when one of the gentlemen identified her as his aunt and pledged his word that she did not want a Parliamentary vote. Her neighbours congratulated her, but in accents that betrayed disappointment. The stir was followed by an expectant hush. The tall man looked steadily at the fingers of the woman in black, which locked and unlocked ceaselessly, though she leaned back in her chair with a vast assumption of unconcern. Those tireless, nervous hands told him what he wanted to know.

The little officious steward was back at his side, whispering in his ear. He shook his head impatiently in reply.

'I'm not going to stay,' he said shortly. 'You've got enough without me, even to deal with two Suffragettes who may not be here; and — well, it's a sickening business, and I'd sooner be out of it.'

He went, and all that was of her world seemed to the woman in black to go with him, as she looked after him, half disappointed, half contemptuous. Up to this point, the Middle Ages were certainly winning, she decided.

The next quarter of an hour was the longest she had ever

lived through. Afterwards, looking back, she remembered every detail of what took place, all the impressiveness of it, all the ironic absurdity. At the time, it felt like holding one's breath for interminable minutes while unfamiliar things went on somewhere in the thick of a mist, as things happen in a bad dream that just escapes the final incoherence of a nightmare.

There was the roar that broke through the mist in a huge wave of sound, when the speakers walked on to the platform. Looking round at that swaying, white-faced multitude, mad with a hero-worship that lost not a jot of its attraction in her eyes because for her there was no hero, the woman in the front row, who had never been to a political meeting before, felt a moment's amazement at her own temerity in coming there, alone with one other, to defy an enthusiasm that had all the appearance of invincibility. Then the mist began to roll away, as somebody started the usual popular chorus. Translated in terms of jolly good-fellowship, hero-worship no longer appeared unconquerable.

To the woman in black it seemed as though a thousand chairs scraped, a thousand throats grated, while the audience settled down, and the chairman delivered carefully prepared compliments, and the great man sorted slips of paper. Then two women, out of the hundred or so who had been admitted because they did not appear to want the historic liberties they came to applaud, clenched lips and hands as the roar burst out once more.

The great man was on his feet, facing it with a gratified smile. To one at least of his audience that smile restored a courage that was in full flight the minute before. That he should strike so egregiously the wrong note, that a fine situation should be met with affability, argued something wrong with the situation or something wrong with the man. There was a false note, too, in that second roar, and it stopped so unexpectedly that one man was left cheering alone in a high, falsetto voice, provocative of instant derision. The fineness had gone out of the situation, and the immediate future of the woman in black, full as it was of unfamiliar fears, came back into some sort of a line with the present.

The absolute silence that greeted the opening period of the ministerial oration had something abnormal in it. It was a silence that almost hurt. The smallest movement put stewards on the alert, made heads go round. The speaker felt the strain, shuffled his notes, stumbled once or twice. Yet, as the tension tightened to breaking-point, the woman in the front row knew the grip over her own nerves to be strengthening by minutes. In the mental commotion around her, she felt the battle already half won that she had come to fight.

A man's voice, challenging a fact, caused a sensation of relief out of all proportion to the slightness of the interruption. Some wag said amiably, 'Turn him out!' and there was laughter. The man, a well-known local Socialist, repeated his objection, and was supported this time by several other voices. There was quite a little stir, and the great man put out his hand benevolently.

'No, no, gentlemen, let him stay!' he adjured the stewards, none of whom had shown one sign of doing otherwise. 'I stand here as the champion of free speech —'

The rest of his sentence was drowned in a spontaneous outburst of applause, during which it was to be supposed that he dealt with the objection that had been raised, for when his words again became audible he had gone on to another point. His next interrupter was a Tariff Reformer, at whose expense he was courteously humorous. The emotional audience rewarded him with appreciative laughter, in which the Tariff Reformer joined good-humouredly. Speaker and listeners were rapidly coming into touch with one another.

The great man, growing sure of his ground, made an eloquent appeal to the records of the past. The woman, who had never heard a politician speak before, leaned forward, hanging on every word. She felt strangely elated, strangely sure of herself, now. This man, believing all that about liberty, seeing all that behind the commonplace of democracy, should surely understand where others had failed even to tolerate. She felt disproportionately irritated by the click of knitting-needles, wondering how any woman could occupy mind and fingers with wool while eternal principles of justice were being thundered over her head. Then there came a pause in the thunder; and sight and sound were blotted out as she took the opportunity, rose to her feet, and stared up blindly at the spot where she knew the speaker to be standing.

'Then give all that to the women,' she said, in a voice she never seemed to have heard before. 'If you think so much of justice and freedom for men, don't keep it any longer from the women.'

For a little space of time, a couple of seconds, probably, her eyes went on seeing nothing, and her ears drummed. She thought she had never known what it really meant to be alone until that moment. She was a woman who had known loneliness very early, when it came to her in an uncongenial nursery; she knew it still, in some houses, where everything was wrong, from the wall-papers to the people. But the meaning of utter isolation she had never learnt until that moment when clamour and confusion reigned around her and she saw and heard none of it.

Then her senses were invaded by the sound and the look of it all; and to her own perplexity she found herself on the point of smiling.

She thought of a hundred things, many of them irrelevant, as she tried in vain to walk to the door, and was obstructed at every step by stewards, who fought to get hold of some part of her in their curious method of restoring order and decorum. She wondered why the meeting was interrupting itself with such complete success, because one woman had made the mistake of thinking that the hero they had welcomed with bad music was a man who meant what he said. She thought of plays she had seen, dealing with the French Revolution, very bad plays most of them, she reminded herself as she was dragged this way and that by excited gentlemen, divided in opinion as to the door by which she was to be ejected. The sea of distorted faces past which they took her, the memory of the knitting-needles, even the intolerable smile of the great man as he made little jokes about her for the amusement of the platform — all this was very suggestive of the French Revolution, as portrayed in a badly written play. In all the plays she had seen, however, she did not remember that there had ever been women who cried a little, or men who sat silent and ashamed, yet not sufficiently ashamed to put a stop to what was going on. These two things appeared to be really happening, here and there among the audience; and she supposed this was why they hurt the most.

She thought of the fastidiousness that made her a jest to her friends, as she felt her hat knocked sideways, looked down and saw the lace at her wrists dangling in rags. The blow that some one aimed at her, as she was dragged unresisting by, seemed a little thing in comparison with those torn strips of lace. Apparently, she was not alone in this eccentric adjustment of proportions; for the little fussy steward who, unbalanced to the point of irresponsibility, had struck the blow, was apologising clumsily the next minute for treading on her skirt. He did not seem to understand when she told him gently that he was the man who had boasted of protecting women since the world began.

Sky and stars looked very remote when at last by circuitous ways they brought her to a door and thrust her out into the night. A final push from the gentleman who liked to see women take an interest in politics, sent her stumbling down stone steps into a moonlit market-place. Everything looked very big, very still, out there, after the banality and the bad staging of the play from which she had just made her unrehearsed exit. In the clearness of thought that came to her, freed at last of hands that dragged at her and voices that coarsened to say things to her that she only now dimly began to comprehend, she knew what it was that had made women, ordinary quiet women like herself, into rebels who were out to fight for the right to protect themselves even against their protectors.

A cheer greeted her from the farther side of the market-place, where the police kept back a crowd that had waited all the evening to see the two Suffragettes from London, and not, as the local paper afterwards somewhat flamboyantly put it, to 'worship from afar the apostle of progress and democracy, almost as the servants of the gods might wait at Olympic banquets for crumbs to fall from the rich man's table.' It was a friendly cheer, she noticed, though this did not matter much. Nothing seemed to matter much, just then, except that the black mass of the cathedral towered overhead and looked unshakeable.

A little altercation floated down to her from the top of the steps, as she leaned motionless against the worn stones of the old balustrade.

'Martha! You of all people! Disgracing me like that! However did you come to be mistaken for one of those screaming —?'

'Well, I couldn't stand the humbug of it, there! Talking about free speech and all that fal-lal nonsense, and then —! I wouldn't let my cat be treated as they treated her, all for nothing —'

'Nothing, do you call it? Coming here on purpose to interrupt —'

'So did that ranting Socialist you think so much of! So did Mr What's-his-name with the husky voice. Why didn't they tear *them* to pieces? Now, you listen to me, James. You brought me here tonight because you said I'd got to be made to think. Very well. I've been made. If you don't like it, you should ha' let me stay at home, as I wanted to.'

She stuffed a mass of dropped stitches into a torn workbag, and went down the steps, her chin in the air. 'If that's politics,' she called back to him from the pavement, 'then it's time women got the vote, if it's only to put a stop to them!'

The girl in grey came round the corner of the building and joined her comrade, who still waited in the shadow cast by the cathedral. Her muff was gone, her cap lopped over one eye, and she held her hand to her throat where the collar had been wrenched at; but her eyes shone with their unalterable courage and spirit. She knew better than any one that every skirmish in the battle they were out to fight was always won before a single blow was struck.

'All right, are you? You did splendidly, for a first shot! Come along to the Martyrs' Cross; the police say we may hold a meeting there. Oh, I know you never have, but you can come and try. Any *idiot* can speak after being chucked out of a Cabinet Minister's meeting!'

Encouraged by this quaint process of exhaustion to regard herself as an orator, the woman who had never been to a political meeting till she went to be·thrown out of one, walked across the market-place to shake hands with the Middle Ages on a spot where men and women were made to die, centuries ago, for having been born too soon.

She found the girl in grey cheerfully assuring an interested crowd that she stood there as the champion of free speech.

Judith Kazantzis

the bath

this dark of which I am the face
this cave beach my canoe finger explores
stretched and ribbed like shipspars

or this cavemouth of water or blood
swamped

drifted anemones out
from my womb to sea
the lost fronds of a cradle unwound

a gentle loss
my finger winds a tiny curl of my leaving

— soft head
birthing myself in bathwater —

shout

she opens her sweet gullible cunt
she wants, a fist
going down into the sweetjar
into the bundle of toffees
she's not lying gurgling
any more: shouting
she wants her fullness
the scarlet doublebeak of a fledgling
crammed

and hoping for that small good world
the inching, aching, sweet, full-up mouth

Alison Fell

Nights

North London 1975

I save my sleeps for when Bill comes. The rest of the
time I get along by way of small strategies not very different
from those used by other women I know who spend nights
alone. I read a lot, new and old books written by women, novels
and autobiographies mainly. Not much theory — I read more
theory when I always slept with Bill. Male novelists don't do,
either, they're too grand, too self-destructive, and I don't like
the way they're always talking about being alone, that compla-
cency, there's something deceitful about it.

Those nights when I know I have to be up early the next day
to take the three children to their two schools, like tonight, or
when I have to catch the bus to work — those are the worst. I
rarely get to sleep before three. So the exhaustion builds
throughout the week, and I let it all out on the nights Bill stays,
clinging to him like a fretful child. (The two boys huddle and
cuddle together every night, demanding nothing of their
parents and everything of each other. If one wakes to go for a
piss, we'll hear the other cry out plaintively for him; the little

girl wakes and goes to her mother's bed promptly every 2 a.m.)
And it darkens early now, since the clocks went back; November
shows in the way the lime trees which shield my window from
craning passers-by lost all their golden leaves in the wind today.

I need light now. Blackness appalls me. Bill fought me for a
year or more before he could accept this. One weekend we borrowed a car and drove to the coast and decided to stay overnight at
Jean's mother's cottage. It was a cold night after a glaring June
day, colder still inside the partly-used cottage, in that clean, neat,
bed-and-breakfast bleakness where all ashtrays. occasional rugs,
electric fires and other homely necessities are battened away in
cupboards. I was already worrying about the light well before
bedtime and by the time we eased ourselves between the chilly
sheets I was panicking; I foresaw conflict about the light and
I foresaw conflict about fucking. No good leaving the landing
light on and the bedroom door ajar — Jean's mother would
stumble out of bed and turn it off; I never could face the prospect
of irritated condemnation from the host in a strange house —
I'd spend long minutes working out how to use a facecloth or
a toothbrush so that it looked as if they hadn't been wetted
and as if I'd brought my own as I imagined proper guests did;
and Jean's mother was a nervous, fussy woman.

So we lay there in the glare of the bedside lamp, staring at
this and that, at the brown shutters, the anaglypta wallpaper,
the black night, the pear tree branch at the window.

'I can't sleep with the light on.' Bill's voice was flat, hating.

'I can't sleep with the light off.'

'I can't bear this.'

'Christ.'

'You know I can't sleep with the light on.'

I could sense Bill's disbelief and hysteria mounting. I am very
afraid of his rages, but I would not give in.

'Why not?'

I started being afraid of men's rage years ago when I slapped
my husband, half-joking, and he floored me with one deadly
serious blow.

'Why not?'

'Jesus if people were meant to sleep with the light on there'd be *no night, would there!*'

'Fucking *what?* Fucking *what?* You'd even bring *God* into it? What an unscrupulous pig!'

Bill gave a hopeless roar and turned away, sobbing slightly. I lay there in the first stage of tears and wavering and want. I stared at the lamp. The fine point of black rage in the middle of my misery only coalesced when an idea came.

'Bastard.'

I jumped up, bouncing the bed as much as possible.

'You won't give in, will you, you won't budge. Look here,' I spat, 'Look at this.' I thrust the bedside lamp under its little table; the embroidered runner hung down in front and the whole room dimmed to an acceptable level.

'You just wouldn't put an *ounce* of creative effort in, would you. You just refused to accept it as a *problem to solve.*' It was so undeniable that although Bill lay there silently for some time with his sullen face saying no no, in the end he couldn't deny it.

Soon after this skirmish he started to keep a small store of candles in his house for my visits.

Perthshire 1950

I was the youngest so I had no choice, they put me in the worst bedroom. Sleeping spiders and the bodies of their flies lurked in the crack where the oily brown wood-panelled walls met the panelling of the ceiling, and the three pines which swayed on a shelf of hill behind my window creaked in each north-east wind which swept down from the moor.

I asked for a nightlight but my father humphed and told me to use my common sense and look at what the walls were made of, and the granary was next door. The Elsan was in the grain-shaft; since my parents and my sister would have had to walk through my room to get to it they kept pots under their beds — so I was the only one who had to use it during the night. That time, I would gladly have been disturbed, I wanted my father's shadowy bulk in its short vest to pad through the room, I would even have welcomed my sister.

51

I clung on to the walls of the grain-shaft as I sat on the Elsan — two rough planks were all that stopped the slopping full container plunging down the black hole into the stables below (*where sewage surged and vipers swam in and out of the iron bars of the mangers ...*) I dug my fingernails deeper into the wood and breathed in quickly. Mice were scratching in the granary. Tomorrow, Sunday, my dad might teach me to shoot; my sister was learning already because she was bigger and stronger.

I jumped off the Elsan without wiping off the wet and fled back through the dark to my camp bed, the click of the metal door latch echoing behind me.

A dull boom sounded from the valley. I shivered. They were blasting again, tunnelling under Bohespic Hill, Polish and Irish workmen from the camp at Dalcroy. My father told me men fell asleep on these endless night shifts; one night someone laid a charge carelessly and a whole mountain loch gushed down and out of the entrance to the tunnel, bringing trout and rubble, silt and toads, grass sods and bodies. My father worked on the hydro-electric scheme too, on machines — diggers and crushers, he called them.

I listened. Two blasts, a smaller one. My father turned over in bed, giving out a wheezing breath, almost a cough. My mother never made a sound in her sleep.

In school holidays I'd cycle down the valley and hang around the camp looking at the strange men and the Chinese cooks, or wander along the shelves of grey granite rubble disgorged by the crusher on the river banks where dust turned the water cloudy-white and gathered in deposits of slimy mud along the shores. The crusher had a coat of white and yellow dust; it towered, menacing and dangerous; one day a man's legs were cut off and my father went to the court in Edinburgh to witness for him when he sued the company.

I listened, poker-stiff and craning, all of a sudden sure that I could hear footsteps coming up the outside rickety stair towards the front door. I strained more — Mrs Thorburn from the farm had been frightened by a man, she said there was a man from the camp gone mad who was walking around naked with staring eyes, so she was keeping Jessie in, but since my mother hadn't said anything and hadn't kept me in I'd forgotten about it.

The noise came again, creak, creak, welling up in my head with the thumping of my heartbeat. He was coming. I tried to count the creaks, each one a step up the wooden stairs, and there were fourteen stairs. He came and came, far more than fourteen steps — I knew he must be taking two steps up, one back, playing and counting in his foreign language with his mad stare, chin stuck out, arms hanging forward with fingers curved to clutch — like the drawings of Paleolithic man in history books. Curved to clutch me, claws curved ...

And it was morning. I haltingly told my mother what I had heard.

'The hens,' she said briskly over her shoulder as she dragged a new calor gas cylinder to the cooker. 'The bantams got loose.' She straightened up, brushing her hair out of her eyes. 'They met me on the top step first thing when I opened the door — silly wee buggers thought they'd get a feed off me, likely.'

Belfast 1972

The corner shop sold potato scones, which I'd loved since I was a child. Alistair did too, I discovered. It also sold expensive packaged coal, sunglasses, balaclavas and red and white flags with the emblem of the Red Hand of Ulster — The Ulster Cross. Every shop window in the Protestant areas was stuffed with this paramilitary regalia. The gasman told us that the street was deserted because the Army was moving families out for their own protection. The curtains in the bedroom at the front of the empty rooming house were floor-length, of crimson sateen — that sateen which has niggling little poly-textured grooves and squiggles; the bed was high, brown and solid, with a counterpane, white with lilac and grey flowers. Into its slippery nylon folds I gasped and sweated my fear as the night events began.

I dozed off for a while, looking at the moon and the

streetlights shining through the chink I'd left in the curtain to serve as my lifeline in the strange soggy dark. I dozed into blankness and then there was *a huge blast*.

'Jesus that was near,' said Alistair as a rattling of windows began and grew — glass was shattering and falling but it was across the street — and eased; the windows held.

'Christ Alistair that was near.' The sounds came out tight and high in a sort of poultry squawk — I felt my head on its stretched neck stuck up absurdly alert from the bed.

'It's late,' he said, 'one a.m.' He stretched to find a Players, lit one for me and put his arm round me, while I waited through his long silence for my cue — I had no idea how to react. I supposed that he did. I hoped dumbly and fiercely that he would stay right where he was, with the dimwittedness of semi-sleep persuading him that the soft bed, the Players smoke and our warm tangled legs were the only reality worth focussing on. I strained to see his profile in the dark. Alistair. That was my chosen name, until I turned out to be a girl.

'Of course you know I'll have to go and take a look, love.' I was starting to say I'll come too we're working together, after all, when the first gunshots crackled. In that frozen moment I had no idea how near or how far they were, I only knew the bed felt much too high, too level with the window sill; exposed, platformed to the skies like an Indian's corpse, I craved the earth, I craved the carpet, I craved the smell of the dust of the carpet in my nostrils.

'Sounds like the Old Park Road.' Alistair walked in front of the window to the wardrobe and dressed himself. He even slipped his reporter's notebook in the pocket of his shiny black mac.

He tried peering through one side of the curtain. As the guns cracked again he leapt back, while I found myself on the floor, on hands and knees, whimpering a bit, glad of the dark which saved me from his eyes.

'They're near — you can see the flashes. It's a heavy gun battle, all right.'

Even if he creeps along in the deepest of the shadows close to the walls, that mac can still catch the light, I thought confusedly, but could get not a word out.

'I'll be back love, I'm very cautious. And I'll not be long, I promise.'

The bedroom door opened and closed softly. The heavy front door thumped shut, leaving me alone in an empty shell of a house, in a depopulated street, in the middle of a war. Paralysed.

Back into bed I crept, back to my cigarettes and my counterpane and my warm familiar body smells. One finger and thumb strayed to the cuff of my hairy old sweater, twiddled the fluff round and round, comforting, comforting: outside, Alistair's frail body was sliding through the dark which had become (had always been, would always be?) murderous. Across the road a child began to cry with a thin hysterical scream Mammy mammy mammy... then I was on the floor again because the guns came again, different guns this time. And the incautious tramp of boots. Shouts of command. The muffled rumble of Saracens. I crossed the rough pile of the carpet caterpillar fashion keeping my head well down until I got to the side of the window. I tweaked the curtain aside and looked — the real scene and my fantasy fitted, apart from a few details. They were slowing down, though, they were stopping; in the centre of the cobbled street they were starring out from the first Saracen, bending double as they raced for the walls, they were throwing up a roadblock *right outside the door*. I jerked my hand away from the curtain and as the last fold swung back into place my eyes filled with an after-image of Armalites sweeping round and up to aim straight at my window. I plunged to the floor. Snipers, they would think, empty house, sniper's gun behind the curtain — shoot first, break the door down.

A hot softness hit my stomach and turned my bowels to liquid and air. An electric rush started up from the base of my spine; my chest constricted; I tried to check it at my throat but I was choking; suddenly it charged my head with dreams and fears from far back in the past.

*War had broken out. In an empty house I ran to answer a
knock on the door, dreading the visitor as I opened it. A soldier
stood there. The machine gun I knew had been waiting for me
aimed unerringly; there was no escape. The first bullets ripped
into me, I fell on the cold tiles of my grandmother's hall, the
jute fibres of the doormat rough against my cheek; there was no
escape from those moments, replayed and replayed.*

They were talking at the front door. A thump. Argument.
Silence. A key *a key* turned in the lock. A remark in a Scottish
accent. Alistair was alive, speaking to the soldiers, thumping
up the stairs, plunging breathlessly into the bedroom.

'Did you hear that? Bastards had me up against the wall ... '
I was alive, I was crawling around the carpet in my knickers.

'I saw them put up the roadblock — did they search you?'

'Oh yes. They were really going to do me over. Christ.' He sat
heavily on the edge of the bed. I crawled back in.

'Were you scared?'

'Petrified.'

'I was crawling ... ' I started, but he broke in.

'God, it was awful, love. The bomb was at the bottom of the
Ardoyne. Provos must have come over the Old Park looking for
whoever laid it.'

Fear made Alistair impotent through all these Irish nights.

Susan Wallbank

If I come

If I come
I'll be more than a hole
for your stick
picking a way through layers
playing my parts
indiscriminately.

If I come
I'll have to bring her with me.
The child.
She comes and goes.
You'll see her
when I laugh too loud
or cry.
She was denied before
and so comes back
for more.

If I come
my mother will come too.
Sometimes silent
often cold
holding back on you.
And father
arthritic now
he cripples me
we use the same bad leg.

Now can you see
why I still hesitate.

For
If I come
I can't come only me
but bring to you
this multiplicity
of we.

Tina Reid

Eye to Eye

The eye shone down on her like a brilliant blue UFO. It was beautiful, celestial; it was one of two. Together they were both invincible, a pair of bobby dazzlers. Lou had examined both many times, though never before point blank. Soon after Mark moved into the house, Lou had taken to sitting up with him a late hour or two almost every night. Just sitting, just talking over the big brown tea-pot in the kitchen that had been hers and Dave's until the joint decision to open up the house, and their lives, a little. While Dave was out at a meeting, or slept exhausted after a meeting, Lou and Mark would explore this and that: fascism and feminism, Lewisham, Grunwick; tea and empathy for two.

Mark had a cool clear voice which elucidated issues and carved precisely round tactics. His voice proceeded from A to B, but his blue eyes danced in counterpoint. They put the flesh on his bony if upright words. Where his tongue was dispassionate, his eyes were compassionate. While his tongue spoke of means, his eyes spoke of ends: warmth and caring, collectivity, creativity, unity and dignity. Oh, it was lyrical. A regular

Rogers and Hammerstein act, these eyes and this voice.

Lou scrutinised again the one eye just now available to her. You wouldn't credit it. There it sailed, lovely, lambent, gentle, serene. The same as ever; and utterly different from what was going on three foot farther down the bed.

Down there, it wasn't so much the thud thud that confounded her. It was more the crooked fingers sunk a good half-inch each into her buttocks. That, and the way her arms were pinned and immobilised by his, not to mention the dead weight pivoted breathtakingly on her thorax. Lou checked it out. The only parts of her body that she herself could operate were her legs from the knees down, but not so as he'd notice. Good God, only last weekend she'd stuffed and trussed a chicken; at least it was dead. Lou groaned and closed her eyes, shut out his, that wreckers' beacon. Her mind sped away like a wheel liberated from a car crash.

This was it. For this Dave, her good comrade and co-parent, had, unasked, in good faith and mortal terror, taken himself off to a weekend conference up North. So that she could practise the theory of relationships they'd arrived at together. So that nothing as crass as his fear would stop it. So that the co-operation between Lou and Mark wouldn't be confined to duplicating leaflets. So that the communication between them need not be checked at the arbitrary frontier of sensuality. And so this person in whom she'd heard a socialist tongue and seen feminist eyes had, invited, occupied her like an imperialist. She couldn't believe it.

Snap. Lou's head cracked back and forth and she was eye to eye with the invader. He'd pulled her upright onto his lap, her legs waggling impotently behind his back as he bounced her vigorously up and down. She had to hang on to his neck for fear of breaking hers. Despite the blur, on the way up and on the way down, Lou caught the warmth and unquestionable honesty in Mark's eyes. He really means it. He's not kidding. Lou's attention skidded back. He thinks we're really making love. He thinks we're really speaking to each other. But he can't possibly hear my body, he's not even listening. He thinks he recognises me, but he's not really looking. He's touching, but he can't feel a thing. Shit! But how can I tell him so's he'll hear, how can I show him so's he'll see? I can't whisper above a din. I can't force gentleness on him. Might as well be a five-foot Asian shouting at a big fat bomber, Stop it, you're hurting me! Napalmed. But before that, those others, the monks, they burned themselves. Yes, that's what you do when you're dissident and powerless. Use what power you have in the one area you control. Self-immolation. Perhaps that's what this was. Perhaps it happened every night throughout the land, millions burning themselves in their beds.

Come on, now, it's only a fuck. Again Lou wheeled back. It's only a fuck with a good kind person she knew well and fancied even better. She must stop being passive, after all she could move her arms now. Lou manoeuvred herself onto her knees, the better to stroke this tender skin, to reach with her mouth his innocent eyes.

Mark sighed, collapsed slowly forward and crushed her legs double. He didn't mean to. He meant well. That was the trouble. That was it. He cared for her and knew what was best for her. Only he didn't know her at all. What's more he didn't know he didn't know, being blind beyond his own eyes, deaf beyond his own noise and numb beyond his own skin. He didn't know that either. He was a Victorian missionary stuck up the Amazon.

Only a fuck, Lou thought viciously, fighting to free her legs. OK, but here is one little end of a long continuum. Or maybe it's the great broad base for the whole pyramid. Love without listening is violent. The giant hand that lifts the mother of toddlers to the nineteenth storey of the tower block is moved by brutal tenderness. It's even possible that in the hearts of those who ravished Vietnam, trembled not only fear of reds, yellows and diminishing markets, but also ignorant love, protective knowing-what-is-bestness. But you need not look so far. Oh brothers, sisters, how many seminal events have you misread in your own beds?

Lou arched her back to release her cramped limbs and Mark

in response kissed her. A few minutes before, in the first tentative fumble before the rough tumble, Lou had smacked these lips, these delicious soft things, with loving relish. Now, a few minutes later, they tasted bad, of her own lies mostly. She couldn't let him in there. She'd had kids. She was used to opening her legs to almost anybody and pretending it didn't mean anything. But she couldn't let him into her head. Not abdicate all responsibility to historical forces. Besides she didn't like it.

Lou gnashed her teeth against his, incidentally biting his tongue and yelled. Mark, wires crossed to the last, roared back, then fell like a stone. Dropped into her crevices as a house settles on its foundations. Cemented together there by sweat and other secretions peculiar to love, Mark heaved for his lost energy and Lou rocked with grief or pity or laughter or anger. In a while Mark opened one incandescent eye. He said, 'I love you.' She said, 'I have to pee.' And who was the more sincere?

Well. She could either lie outright, or mumble deceptively and pretend to fall asleep. Or she could say the kids were moaning and hadn't she better lie down with them for a bit. Or she could do the right thing, tell the truth, even unsolicited and then try to explain it all. Protect and educate, those were the watchwords of constructive criticism. But oh god, Marx, Reich, someone, what a job! First the bewilderment, then the hurt, then the anger. It would be like an action re-play of her own just past experience, only in much slower motion. There'd be empathy to push past too; he wouldn't be the only one in the bed ever to have felt 'sexually inadequate'. And he'd never see what it had to do with the GLC or the Pentagon. There just isn't the vocabulary. It was too bloody much. It would take all night and the baby woke at 6.30. It would take weeks, with her, the victim, licking his wounds. Lick them she'd have to if there was to be any hope for the relationship. Poor thing.

There was a nasty groove round her bum when she finally left the lavatory, refused the impulse to poke the baby awake, and slid back into bed beside Mark. He was fast asleep. Lou slid out again.

Running away to her own bed, chickening out, just like a chick, trussed chicken; in the morning she could always say that thing about the kids crying. That's all she'd say. Dave would come back, possibly never to lie easy in his bed again, but convinced of a small shuffle forward. Mark would stay ignorant, intact; though, rejected, the small imperialist within would grow stonier. And she was a coward for sure. Must get a couple of hours before the baby gets up. Jerked alert by a rustle that could have been defoliant over the forest, or Mark's feet on the landing, but was only rain down the chimney, London rain; if I can't take on this little struggle in my territory, my person, with such a small and well-disposed opposition, what about the revolution? Maybe that was easier. There, there was solidarity. Here, the only possible solidarity was between opponents. Fucking hell!

Fucking hell, then the whole household slept for a bit.

Amiya Rao

Uma

Uma died last night. As in life, so in death, she made no fuss. We knew she was not keeping good health, but then we also knew from the doctor whom we had called once, that there was nothing very special about her illness. It was the usual disease — whatever that may be — that females suffer from after repeated childbirths; and after all she was twenty-six and no longer young. We never bothered. I had my hot cup of tea at six in the morning, my hot lunch at nine sharp — for I had to catch the 9.45 UP-Calcutta train every day. My aunt's Puja utensils shone like gold, our cow Budhi and her calf were fed in time, children bathed and looked after and rooms swept and kept tidy. The daily routine was never upset; nor were we.

I was having my after-dinner game of chess, as I did every night at the Board's office, when our maidservant came to call me. 'Bohudidi is ill, Mataji wants you.' Mataji was my mother and Uma, after twelve long years of married life, was still the Bohudidi — the sister. I was in the middle of the most exciting game — my Queen was in trouble. I finished it and left for home. From the road, the little house looked completely

normal, all wrapped up in sleep. The big moon was up, right
on top of the house and the shadows of the Deodar fell long and
black. There was not a sound, but no, wasn't that lame pet dog
of Uma's whining somewhere? And there was one thing more
rather unusual for this time of the night: the kerosene lantern
was burning in the little storeroom where Uma had lately
taken to sleeping. When I came home, my mother and my aunt
were out on the porch. Uma was already dead.

Then the friends were called and Uma was dolled up in her
wedding sari. Mother quietly removed her two worn-out earrings and her single gold bangle, both her parents' gifts. Her
feet and forehead were daubed in the vermilion of married
women and she was ready for the last lap of her journey. I went
in to have a last look at her — or was it the first time I ever saw
her! The tired, drawn face, now rested; the long lashes almost
touching the upper cheek, the little dip in the chin, the thin
short nose and the curve of the lips. Was it Uma — the girl I
had married? I looked on fascinated. The lame dog moaned
just outside the window; how did it know? Children slept on in
another room. Someone laughed outside under the mango
tree. Mother and aunt were consulting the priest about the
auspiciousness or otherwise of the moment of her death.
Somebody was chopping some wood; more people were
coming; through the window they looked like so many legs and
dangling lanterns. And someone entered the room; it was the
head of the village, whom I call uncle. He embraced me
warmly and comforted me: 'Don't worry son, she was the true
Sati [legendary ideal wife]. She has served you well, given you
sons, finished her allotted task on this earth and gone to
Heaven. But the house cannot remain empty for long. We shall
soon get you another Lachmi [auspicious bride].' Mother and
aunt grunted their approval and Uma slept on looking ridiculously young in her red Benarasi sari.

Then the arrangements were complete and Uma was lifted
out of the wooden bed and put on the rope charpoy and carried
outside, head towards our house, never to return again. Where
the village ended and the river began, a fire was lighted and

the flames leapt up and took Uma. Soon there was no Uma, but just a little dust. Soon that too wasn't there, for the Ganges took it.

The moon hung low down in the Chhatim trees, heavy with sleep, and the east was mellow with the birth of dawn. I returned and went into the small storeroom. It looked as it always did. On the wall hung the tiny old mirror, its frame nearly gone; in the niche beside it stood the little pot of vermilion. Behind it were the few discoloured hairpins, a piece of black ribbon and an old medicine bottle half full of coconut oil. On the ground, against the wall, stood the cheap, tin box. What did it hold, what precious treasures of its mistress? It had no lock and held no secrets. There were a few cotton saris, neatly folded; under them was a green silk sari, now ten years old, but almost new; under the sari was a photograph carefully wrapped in a big, white handkerchief: a shy little bride in a red Benarasi sari and her young bridegroom in white muslin looked up at me from behind the glass. Right at the bottom of the trunk was a tiny chintz dress and a pair of childrens' bangles. I knew them all. The green silk sari was bought in a moment's indiscretion, the day I had a rise from Rs50 to Rs70. I was at my desk like every day when the Manager himself came up to our line of desks and announced the great news. All six of us rose from 50 to 70, in one day. To celebrate, I bought some cauliflower and Simla peas, a bottle of Kashmere honey, a big rubber doll for Maya, a pair of canvas shoes — and then suddenly I saw the sea-green sari in a pavement shop and bought it. I had almost missed the 7.15 down, that evening. Late at night, she had put it on. The little chintz dress and the chipped glass bangles had no story to tell. Maya, the little one who owned them once, had herself become a story. The song came back, the lullaby:

Come on dream fairy, come oh come,
Bring sleep for my darling — sweet, my lotus eyed Maya.

Both were asleep today, mother and daughter.

I took the photograph out and sat on the floor, looking at the little bride and her bridegroom. The past came out of the sea of oblivion. There sat the foolish pair, on that very wooden bench; she lost in the folds of her voluminous Benarasi sari, and he in white muslin, a garland of jasmines round his neck. Their first night together.

I woke up with a start, the sun was on the wall, a new day had begun. I put the photograph back and shut the tin box. The house was long awake; mother was grumbling: her Krishna-Radha lamp had no oil in it. Aunt was muttering: 'Not fair, not fair at all; how can one cook at this age ... ' Budhi was bellowing heavy with milk, she could not understand what was wrong that morning. Children were shouting for Ma and breakfast which was long overdue. I was in a panic, for the 9.45 UP-Calcutta had come and gone. The lame dog alone lay quietly by the storeroom window, its ugly face between its thin legs. But that is because the brute had not heard the comforting news of my aunt's sister-in-law's niece reaching just the 'ripe age' ...

Astra

too late

it's too late, mother,
for you to know
i think of you
and often see
your face   your form   your wrinkles
  (which were few)
in other round small women
in the roads and streets

i have needed all this time to know
you were right
in denouncing family
(as an institution, not certain individuals —
for you hurt a lot of feelings)
in chafing at the role of mother
(i recognise the resentments)
in writing in green and purple inks
(i do the same sometimes)
in pasting silver stars on your letters to me
when i was little and when i was grown
(to cheer me up or yourself?)

i used to think you
childish   eccentric   frivolous
but now i know
you were on the right track
though i can't say what that was
only that i love you for it all
now:
too late

you died alone in your sleep
in your salvation army room that I never saw
because you were ashamed, i guess

and now my tears wet this paper
and my biscuits burn in the oven

Stef Pixner

O-U-T Spells Out

    She arrived one day to live across the street from us.
I watched her from the window.

'Mum, a new girl's come to live in our road. Shall I go and
ask her to play with me?'

'Leave it a couple of days, Brenda, give them a chance to
settle in.' I watched her with my nose pressed against the glass.
But I didn't wait. Creeping shyly out of our flat, I knocked on
her front door.

'Do you want to come out and play with me? I've got a new
skipping rope ... ' That's how we met. Skipping:

> *A house TO let*
> *no rent TO pay*
> *knock at THE door*
> *and run Away.*

We saw each other every day. On the way to school, and on
the way back. When she was ill I dragged myself there alone, I
didn't want to go without her. She was a year older than me,

with green eyes and goofy teeth and wispy brown hair. We trailed off to school, kicking leaves and climbing walls. I was scared and she laughed at me. 'Scaredy cat, scaredy cat.' So I tried harder, until I could skip along the tops. We were often late, and on the way home we used to stop at a cafe and spend our pocket money on cups of strong tea and pretend we had husbands and children and had to make do on £11 a week.

One day she was ill and couldn't go to school. So I pretended I was ill too. Mum went out to buy blackcurrant juice and paraffin for me, but I thought she'd gone out to work. So I rolled up my pyjama bottoms, pulled on a skirt and jumper, and went over the road. We'd been playing for a couple of hours when there was a heavy banging at the door. It was Mum, her eyes red from crying. She thought I'd been carried off and she was just about to phone the police. She dragged me out by the arm and slammed the door. She dumped me into bed and went off to work and I sat in the dark as a kind of penance. After that I wasn't allowed to see Pat for several weeks. I did of course. There was no way of stopping me. We swore we'd be friends for ever, and that in a year or two we'd run away from home and travel round the world, working our passage, or as stowaways.

Some months after that incident had blown over, I stayed the night at her flat. It was exciting and we talked and giggled till late into the night. Her mother kept shouting at us to be quiet or I wouldn't be allowed to stay there again. So I got into her bed and we whispered and buried ourselves under the bed-clothes so her Mum couldn't hear when we exploded with laughter. When it was very late we did quieten down. We were trying to keep each other awake; she was blowing in my ear, and I was tickling her feet. Then we hugged each other.

'You're my best friend,' I said.

'So're you,' she replied. My heart was beating and I felt funny. I pressed myself against her and she responded by holding me tight.

'Promise you'll never tell anyone,' I said.

'Promise.'

We just lay there, pressing tight against each other with our hearts beating like mad.

The summer after that we went away at different times in the holidays. We wrote often at first, about everything that was in our hearts. But towards the end of the summer she didn't write much. I just counted the days till she got back. But when she did get back, something had changed. She was different. I rushed over to see her as soon as I could but she was snooty and cool. I stayed and stayed trying to think of the right thing to say, until I heard mum calling me, and I slunk off home. I tried again a few more times, and I asked her what had happened, but she was superior and sarcastic and laughed at the things we'd shared and made me feel a fool. She didn't want to climb walls anymore and she gave her mice and goldfish away. She started wearing nylons and lipstick and reading grown-up novels. She didn't want to go to school with me in the mornings because, she said, I made her late. She was writing to someone. I knew because I saw her post the letters and I watched her wait for the postman in the mornings. I wished I was dead. Or rather I liked to imagine my death in a film. I would get ill and waste away and she would finally come and see me when it was too late. Or, my eyes blurred with tears, I would have an accident. Then she'd be sorry. Then she'd remember our love.

But the months passed, and I found other friends. It wasn't the same, but things weren't so painful any more. I stopped watching her front door hour after hour with my nose pressed against the glass. We even began to say hello again when we saw each other in the street. And then I heard from Mum that she was leaving London, she was going away with her family to live in another town. I waited for the next holidays to come, and then creeping shyly across the road, I knocked on her door.

She answered with a straight face and let me in. We began to talk a bit, awkwardly. We played some records, and she gave me my first cigarette. We talked about boys. She'd stopped writing to the boy she met on holiday. She said he was boring and she couldn't remember what he looked like anymore.

Anyway there were several more she had in mind.

'How about you?' she asked me.

'Oh, lots,' I lied, just watching her, just wanting.

'I've got new clothes to go away with,' she said. 'Come and see.'

So I went into her room again and we sat down on the pink candlewick bedspread. We didn't say a word, though sentences came into my mind and I rehearsed them, trying to make them sound natural. I could see us reflected in the big mirror which stood on her chest of drawers. There were little glass animals in front of it on a lace mat, and pictures from magazines stuck on the walls. Past the mirror and the net curtains was the street. The silence went on and on. In the end, I reached out my hand. She was still at first, but then she leaned over and laid her head on my shoulder. We stayed like that for a long time, and although her hair was tickling my chin, I didn't dare to push it away. Then I hugged her tightly, my heart thumping like before, and my hands sweating. I pulled myself away.

'I've got to go now,' I said. 'Promise you'll write.'

'Yes,' she said. But she never did.

dip dip dip
my little ship
sails across the water
like a cup and saucer
O-U-T spells OUT.

Ann Oosthuizen

Bones

Looking back, the experience seemed to her like a collection of brightly polished beads, or because they were about death, like bones picked clean of flesh, eroded by sun and wind. She tried to fit them together to form a sequence, a skeleton of meaning, but they remained singular, isolated moments clearly cut away from the blank, dead time that surrounded them. Why she remembered these moments and not others, or indeed why events happened thus and not otherwise, she was at a loss to understand, but each remembered incident was carved in her mind, hard and clear, like an image in whitened bone. She sat, like a witch-doctor, throwing these bones, over and over, to find their meaning.

The blanket they had covered him with was green. It was the sort of lurid green that is used to dye cheap blankets. She knew this because she and Stephen had owned two such blankets, bought during the first years of the marriage. In fact, at the time she had thought the men had taken one off the beds to cover him, but it turned out subsequently that those two were still in place. She shut her eyes and saw them pass with the stretcher. They had not looked at her as they moved him down the stairs and out of the front door. She stood silently in the open doorway not knowing how to say goodbye to what they carried. She could recall this scene at any time; two faceless men with the lumpy stretcher under the green blanket.

She had waited in the street because she could not bear the silence which surrounded him. 'Why have you taken so long?' she cried to the doctor and ran up the stairs. But Stephen was already blue. 'Mrs Craig, he has gone. Your husband is dead.' She lifted her hands.

She stood at the window while the doctor telephoned. The window was large, divided into squares by strips of white wood and the deep sill was also white. She looked out on a street which was already autumnal, showing the first flurry of dry leaves, although the dying year was yet just a hint in the warm wind. 'He had so much to do!' she repeated. His death was unbelievable. The world had turned into a nightmare where the impossible happened. The doctor said, 'Mrs Craig, you are very calm,' and gave her some yellow pills.

There was suddenly nothing for her to do. Early the next morning, long before the ragged army of black workers who serviced the white town, the cleaners, milkmen, gardeners, postmen and delivery boys passed her window, her son, Jeremy, came to her bed. They lay silent, cold, their bodies not touching, waiting until it would be time to get up. They lay in the big, empty double bed waiting for an excuse to start the day.

The wife of the Professor of Music lent her six black hats, but she put on a black veil which was also borrowed. On the way down to the car, turning the bend in the stairs, Jean saw her neighbour staring up at her in horror. She and her husband had been away for the weekend and had just returned. 'Jean!' she cried. Jean walked as if in slow motion down the stairs, her hand on the balustrade, dressed in black for her husband's funeral. She felt as if she were watching a film and playing a part in it, both acting and watching, observed and observing.

The pills had helped, she supposed, but it was more than that, it was a disbelief in the reality of what was happening. The disbelief was so total that when the Vice-Chancellor stumbled charmingly across the lawn to offer condolences, she could stand up and be charming to him too. It was more than disbelief though, it was that this death had called into question her whole relationship with the world she lived in. Where did she fit in now? Who were these people? They were his friends, his students, his colleagues. They had honoured him. She watched the endless procession of cars driving behind them to the cemetery, she noticed, but did not see, the people crowded around the grave. She had been Stephen's wife. What were these people to her? But a more important question was; what was she to them? If she cried, how long would they hold her? It was safer not to ask. It was safer to endure.

She watched them all climb into motor cars and drive away. Jeremy and she were left behind, standing on the sunlit pavement with the house at their backs, the front door open to receive them. They were part of the parameters of Stephen's life, no more than his books, his pipes, his furniture, his house, his car, his clothes. Together they made up a collection without an owner, although she was to become a self-appointed caretaker of all his goods. Where was Stephen? To them he was still in all those things, or rather he still claimed those things and they were answerable to him — for his house, his car, his books, his garden. She had not known then how much other people would want to own his possessions, perhaps sharing her respect for the meaning he had attached to them. She had not known then how bitter she would become in defending them. She and Jeremy accepted his valuation of those objects, loved them because he had collected them, feared losing them because they feared his displeasure. They wanted everything to stay the same, even their own lives still belonged to him.

Looking back on the experience now, with some irony, it seemed obvious that they had been busy defending a tomb. The vultures came and they beat them off, but the tomb had no life in it. This was what gave each image its bitter poignancy, what made her grimace as she recalled each scene and the emotion that went with it. Yet she remained chained to these bones, these memories, searching for the right clue that would click them into place and free her from them.

She was accosted in the bank, at the side counter where you ring for statements. It was Mrs Lewis, a small woman with restless jerky movements, brown hair trimly waved. Pressing herself up close against Jean's body, her little beaver face quivering with eagerness, her brown eyes darting over Jean's face, she said, 'Oh, Jean, I know it is rather quick' — it was in fact only four days since the funeral — 'but we are really interested, we wondered if you would be selling your plot on the coast. Are you thinking of staying on here?' The earth rocked under her feet. Her hands went out to steady herself on the bland wood counter. 'No,' she managed to reply.

Oh, the sea, where they had spent so many days in the golden times, driving there even when Jeremy was quite small. They had slid down sand dunes, gaily, on red and blue plastic toboggans, made fires on the beaches, sung songs in the lamplight, driven home sticky from the salt wind and the warm sun. They had bought the plot to build on, had paced it, fenced it, heard the sea beat in their dreams and the dunes stretch out in warm embrace.

'You will let us know if you ever think of selling, won't you?'

Jean stood firm, defending their land. With Stephen no longer there as protector, it seemed that everything he owned was up for grabs. Jeremy would sit on the floor next to the telephone, on guard, when the estate agents called. 'We have a buyer, we were wondering if you would be needing such a big house now. We were wondering if you would like to sell.' 'No.' 'And of course, there is your plot at the sea.' 'No.' Why did she have to put up with this now? The world thought they were fair game, but they would be cunning and strong. They kept the house and the land, jealously, not for themselves, but for him. They were holding on to what he had left, what they had left of him.

The front door bell rang. It was the old black man who came

77

regularly for money. 'The Master always gave me money, I have come to ask you for some.' She stood with her back to this enormous double-storied house, crammed full of furniture and books and clothes and felt like the captain of a sinking ship. How could she save all this, how would they survive now without Stephen who had chosen, paid for and maintained all these possessions, including herself and Jeremy? All her fears found focus in this one black beggar, standing thin and frail at her door. 'Have you no mercy?' She screamed at him, her rage turning him from victim to persecutor, herself into the poor widow. 'If he had pity for you, have you no pity for his widow?' He started to edge away from this hysterical white woman. 'Will you always take? Will you never give something?' She raved, beside herself with self-pity. He moved carefully behind the white gate. 'I am going now, I am sorry.'

Rudderless, she stood at Stephen's cupboard; his clothes still carried his smell. She held a black sweater in her hands and put it to her face. How can a man's smell live longer than the man himself? She wore it and carried the smell with her, but after it was washed the smell was yet another memory. His shoes, with garden soil still on them, stood empty. Jeremy wore his socks and later his shirts and jackets. They gave nothing away. A colleague wrote, could he have the academic gown, in memory, he would wear it in memory. A dealer in old clothes at the door was politely disbelieving when she said she had nothing to sell. The siege went on, a young black man had once borrowed *The Rise and Fall of the Dutch Republic*, could he have it? Her sister-in-law, visiting the bereaved family, asked to buy the big rococo cupboard and eyed Stephen's typewriter. 'Jean, do you need them?' she was asked. She stifled her rising panic. No, she did not wish to sell, she was not leaving the house. No, the seaside plot was not for sale. There would be no change ...

The envelope addressed to her lay on the mat, the name on the account had been changed from Mrs Stephen Craig to Mrs Jean Craig. She had liked the title, Mrs Stephen Craig. It had allowed her to share the power of his position, gave her the same social status that he occupied. She was still the same person. She still felt married to him. Mrs Stephen Craig had been acceptable and proper when he was alive, why not now that he was dead? Yet it did not matter how many times she corrected the accounts, they came back inexorably, Mrs J., Mrs Jean. However hard she fought, Stephen was being taken away from her. Or was it Stephen? Was it not that she feared losing this image of herself as Stephen's wife? If she lost that, what would be left? She had made him her shield and had hidden behind him for so long that she could no longer see herself as a separate person, but she had no choice, she was forced to step out of his shadow. Mrs Jean Craig was born, as we all are, without our permission, even unconscious of the meaning of our birth. Later she was to hear the title Ms, but it came too late for her, she had by that time rejected all titles, Ms, Miss, Mrs, were all one to her, confused between her father's name and her husband's, taken on marriage, she had become simply Jean. Jean Who? She did not know. Perhaps it was too late to find out. She threw the bones, looking again for images, trying to link experience to form patterns, meaning.

The car skidded on the untarred road. It was New Year's Day, the height of the summer drought and the road's surface, smoothed away by holiday cars, was treacherously pitted with small holes and jutting stones. She drove fast. It was hot and after weeks at the sea, she and Jeremy, their skins salty, their toes etched in black by the river sand, their hair thick and bleached with salt and sun, were returning home because of a message given to the seaside shop that their house had been broken into during the night.

They talked anxiously about what could have been taken. This had never happened before and they had no idea what the burglars wanted. Would they take clothes? Jean had not feared for her own, but for his, those unworn suits and jackets, empty shoes, his dressing gown behind the bedroom door, but it was not clothes the burglars had come for, they took what they could carry quickly away in their pockets, small things that could be given away or sold and among them were treasures, not in value, but for those two anxious people.

Broken glass and splintered wood from the kitchen window lay on the floor. There was candle-wax on the stairs. Drawers lay open, their contents hurriedly spilled out. What was gone? The police and insurance wanted lists, but it was only later, during moments of conversation, pausing in mid-sentence to check each beloved object, that she discovered what was missing; his watch, carefully kept for when Jeremy was older, his grandfather's gold pocket watch, long since broken, which he had valued. How could other people need them as they did? She bit her lip, controlling her anguish. She could not guard it all, accountable to Stephen's memory for each new loss.

From then on the house became a target for the small, homeless boys who scavenged the streets and lived in the storm drains beyond the large gardens. Stephen had built Jeremy a tree-house in an old pepper tree in the far corner of the lawn. It was small and dark, and Jeremy had not made much use of it. The neighbours complained that vagrant black children were using it for shelter at night. It was useless to send the children home, young as they were, they were largely on their own, the poverty of their homes could not feed them and the houses in the black part of the town were even more overcrowded than the nine foot square box in the pepper tree. She took the roof off the tree-house to discourage the children from camping on her land. It was preferable to calling the police.

But the children had become familiar with the house and knew the way in. The house had always stood open, yet now, if the kitchen door was unlocked, the food in the refrigerator, cheese or meat, would disappear in a flash. Even when she was at home the big French doors onto the garden, the kitchen door, the front door all had to be locked. They were living in a fortress. Slowly an aversion to the house grew in her. They guarded too much. They had too much.

How had this happened? Jean looked back on those days remembering how she had slammed shut the door of the empty fridge muttering angrily and impotently, 'Property is theft!' She was being forced to consider her relationship to all the contents of the house. She did not yet feel trapped, served unquestioningly the master whose unspoken commands she had framed for herself, yet she rebelled at the thought that she must be forever answerable to a dead man for the things he had owned, cleaning his silver, locking his doors. What had she to do with all this fine furniture, the lovely garden, the roses nodding on the marble table, the polished wood gleaming silkily in the candlelight? Stephen Craig was dead. Yet although she and Jeremy clung out of fear to an identity which had given them the only security they knew, he could no longer help her work out her confusions, she could no longer follow his lead, expect him to make the moral decisions which would carry them through the next stage in their lives. In the past, Stephen's presence in their lives had meant that at any time they knew who they were by their relationship to him and Stephen had always seemed to know who he was. He had also made it clear who he expected them to be and Jean admired him and feared his disapproval even then, after his death.

She searched for another moment in time which had made her, Jean, move away, out of the security of her husband's shadow into the wind and space of a whole person. Even now she could not talk of an identity, perhaps she would never find that, but she was beginning to know what she was not. And she was no longer Mrs Stephen Craig. How had this happened?

They stood inside a small wooden house, one room, ten foot square, while outside the dry cold wind blew up stinging gusts of sand and rocked the walls. They had driven two hundred miles to gather information on a resettlement camp. That there were camps, solitary communities of displaced, exiled and homeless people living in houses put up neatly, but without hope on the open veld, was just beginning to be publicly acknowledged and, as Stephen's widow, she was a likely choice of companion to this small party of whites who wished to see for themselves what such a place was like. They had eaten a large lunch with the Roman Catholic priest who was now showing them round his parish. In the house lived a young woman whose husband was contracted to work for a construction business 800 miles away.

A small wood fire burned in the centre of the room. There was no chimney and the fire gave off little heat, although smoke was everywhere. Two children, both under five years, sat huddled round it, while a third lay asleep on the only bed. He did not wake when the party of five adults entered the house. There was no floor, but the dry earth swept clean and the only furniture was the bed and four wooden boxes covered in clean newspaper on which stood two empty cooking pots. The house was painfully tidy, but gave off the same air of exhaustion that was apparent in the little boy asleep on the bed.

The priest asked the woman where her husband was. For the benefit of the visitors he interpreted her reply. She looked sadly at them; he was in Cape Town, she saw him for three weeks each year. He had not seen the baby she had conceived on his last visit and which she now carried on her back. Standing there, unable to make the least difference to a situation that she found intolerable, Jean wanted to say to this woman that she knew what it was like to manage a home without a husband, that she understood, that she had suffered too, but the words choked in her throat in that desolate room.

They walked to the car which was parked outside on the dusty road, the cold wind catching at their heavy coats, leaving behind them a woman alone. Jean knew she had failed, knew that there are moments in our lives when we must, like Job, tear our clothes and cover our bodies with ashes and that this had been such a moment. She walked back to the glass and chrome car and let them drive her home to the big house that she locked to keep safe all those thing which had been entrusted to her care.

And she saw herself a prisoner. In accepting Stephen's valuation of all the beautiful things he owned, in caring for them and protecting them, in insisting that her life now was in no way different from a life which had ended with Stephen's death, she had locked herself into the house and into his death. She had made it impossible for herself, Jean, to react immediately as one woman to the life of another. Who had appointed her caretaker to this collection of lovely objects owned by a dead man? It was herself, unable to take possession yet holding on to a style of life which was so far from what she was feeling.

The silence around his body was complete. She could summon it back at any time, hear it and feel the fear. She had to get back to that. It was a silence which did not reproach. It was beyond that. All their busy manning of the house had been a response to his life and what they had understood as his life. They had never understood his death. She moved gingerly into the void, dying in life.

And made her will. If she were to act she must leave things tidy. It was her first step into the unknown and also her first responsible action. She gave her lawyer her power of attorney and she applied for two passports, one for herself and one for Jeremy. She was separating herself from him so that her actions would be those of one person only. She did not want to involve him in her decisions, she had learned enough to know how easy it is to make another person your accomplice by dominating his spirit. From now on she and Jeremy were separate. They would make separate decisions, they had no common identity. That they loved each other was understood, they were gentle with each other, but they no longer worked as a team following the commands of an unseen general. She was spinning into space, her route uncharted, she would make no decisions for Jeremy, but she would make sure that he was safe.

The town was in crisis. Six thousand people were told they would be moved from their homes, not to alternative housing in the town, nor with adequate compensation for their loss, but to a barren site on the high bank of the Fish River, twenty miles away. It was not a new crisis, the threat of removal had hung over the people in the township for over ten years, but now the plans seemed imminent. She could not stand outside these events. She knew she must fight with the same determination with which she had defended her own home. Yet how could she act from the safety and comfort of this, the white side of the town? She could see the township every morning as she looked out of her bedroom window. Even from a distance it was mean and squalid, the tiny houses jumbled together on a bleak hillside. The different government departments said the eviction was slum clearance. The two black men in her sitting room looked at her in sullen rage, let them do it then, was all they would say, we have been threatened long enough, they might as well move us, we are already dead.

She drove out to the site of the new resettlement camp. It was a twenty mile ride along a road which led to nowhere in particular. She walked the barren land, saw the grey shale which covered the surface of the earth so that only small stunted cactus and tiny, tough rock plants grew there. No preparations were being made for the sudden influx of 6,000 people, the spot was deserted, there was no life there at all.

She began to write letters, call meetings. The Minister said the township would have all modern amenities, it would have schools, community centres, flush toilets, work. She formed a small committee; one of its members called it Auntie Jean's action group; they wrote again; what assurance could the Minister give that people would not be moved before such amenities were available? Everyone knew his promises were ludicrous. The different government departments never met, so could not even formulate a coherent plan. The Water Board said it was unlikely there would be water on the site for at least ten years, when various enormous and expensive irrigation projects were completed. The City Council was hoping to get rid of 6,000 people to ease the burden of unemployment in the city, not caring what would happen to the families that were moved. She was part of this struggle. She had fought for her own home. She knew what it meant to be threatened like this.

It was increasingly difficult to ignore the view from her window. Working for a charitable organisation, she visited an old man who received from them a little extra on his pension, a ration of dehydrated soup and mealie meal. It had been raining and the yard outside his house was full of muddy puddles. She picked her way through the dirt to his front door, which leaned precariously open. He lay on the ground in that damp house, coughing from bronchitis, covered in sacks. It amazed her that he answered her list of questions courteously.

When a visitor to the town praised its charm and beauty, she answered, 'You should visit the other side. You should see the location.'

She began to make connections between the way she lived and the poverty across the valley. She was asked to speak at a local girls' school. The older girls sat in a big hall, ranged in front of her. She perched informally on the table which had been set up for her, hoping to break the distance between herself and them, not wanting to use her age as a weapon. It was the first time she had spoken in public and she was very nervous. She had spent some time on what she wanted to say and she read each word of what she had prepared. She wanted to make sure that the girls would understand their own complicity in the poverty that edged all their lives. She spoke about the way she saw the rich and poor as connected. 'When we truly wish to make a better world, we have to admit these connections,' she said. She said that the girls must realise that it was not their own merit, nor that of their parents, that had made their education possible, but that they were at this expensive school precisely because one out of every four babies died in the location. She had wanted to push them into action, but she had not been prepared for the anger and hostility which exploded when she finished. Girls sprang up from all over the hall, they said that black people were stupid and lazy and dirty and had themselves to blame for their own poverty. They drank too much and had too many children. No one asked what she could do to change things. As she prepared to leave, one girl apologised to her privately, 'You see,' she said, 'you attacked us personally.' Later she heard that she would not be allowed to speak again at the school. The girls had been so upset that night that there was an uproar in the dormitories.

There was no one to talk with. Stephen's friends were embarrassed if she spent too much time with them. She was a single woman now and might mistake friendship for something more. Their wives talked endlessly about their husbands and children, making her uncomfortable. She felt isolated by their structured lives. She was invited to 'family' picnics with the children, rather than to the adult social occasions where the men sat and talked together while their wives made tea. When she had been hostess at Stephen's parties, her opinion was respected by his friends. Now she was considered too abrasive, too extreme. Perhaps she was becoming so.

She and the house were like a whale beached on the shore, dying. She longed for tenderness, for a strong arm to hold her, comfort her and take her burden from her. Her body ached with loneliness. There is a special pain we feel after a loss which catches us in the centre of our body, making us double up in agony over the emptiness inside us. She was not allowed to reveal her need. And the house made no sense any more. She made plans to leave it. She both loved and hated each treasured object. She still cut roses for the blue and white patterned vase, still oiled and rubbed the golden wood, satin with age, but the house no longer represented who she was. It stood for the past, its opulence combined both comfort and culture, yet she knew that its quiet good taste was only the reverse side to poverty. It was the harvest gathered by her white colonial ancestors from that arid hillside which she saw from the height of her bedroom window, a hillside criss-crossed with paths made by the feet of all those underpaid and underfed generations who shared a common colonial history with her. As she stood at her window staring at the dip in the hill where the ground was ash grey, the town rubbish dump, she could see grey figures scrabbling in the smoking ash for anything worth using. One hundred years ago, the angry tribes had come over that hill, daring under the leadership of a great general to pit their spears against the British guns. She had been taught that their defeat was a victory for civilisation, had seen the monument erected to the white woman who braved the savage Impis to bring gunpowder to beleaguered white soldiers. She felt angry and cheated that her whole life had been so rotten with lies. Her home was beautiful, beyond anything she had seen elsewhere, but it was a lie. It was a monument to oppression, there was no beauty here. She must go away.

If she came back she would do so under another flag.

At what moment did she say goodbye to the vision of life which had defined her until this time? An image of sequence surprised her; it gave a new direction, changed the pattern.

She could see herself sitting in the window of the farmhouse in which she had grown up. The view was tremendous; close by were the flower-beds and lawns round the house, on the left the road led to the river which was flanked by tall poplars and scrubby thorn trees, and in the distance the vast Karroo mountains were solid blue against the open sky. It had been to a different Jean, another self that she had said her most painful goodbye. Looking for the Jean who had existed before her marriage, before she had taken on the roles of wife, mother, caretaker, she had gone back to the place where she had spent her childhood. She had needed to understand a time when she had been herself alone, a time before she had become an addition to Stephen's life.

Her fingers clutched the imaginary bones; find the pattern, evoke the moment. Jeremy was with her. They had gone to say goodbye. The journey to the farm had taken three hours and she was tired, too tired to climb the river cliff as she had always done on such visits, her body incapable of the effort. She sat at the window and looked out on the landscape of her childhood; this was the place where she had wandered alone along the dry river bed, walked between tall rocks, climbed to the eagle's nest. This was where she had sat stalking turtles in the muddy water, where she had run from a cobra curled silently under the piece of tin which covered the old well, all that was left of a windmill which had been swept away in a flood before she was born. She had loved each tree, each crevice, unconscious of how much she had loved because she had had no sense of her own consciousness. Who was that Jean? She could not see herself, yet remembered clearly each stone and tree, each warm smell. She felt the sunlight on her brown skin, the sudden pain of a thorn in her bare foot. When she searched for herself she found only feelings, sensations, visions, not a child who was aware that she was growing into a woman. The farm was stocked with Victorian and Edwardian love stories, yet the child who read avidly the romantic literature of the past never saw herself in the mystical role of Woman. She had been unconscious of any destiny for herself, accepted a society in which she would play no major part. The child, who had read about and admired the bravery of others, never saw herself as a heroine. That child had become servant, slave, lieutenant, never Goddess. This was no wonder, thought the seeker, when she was the child sitting quietly in the sun, letting others shape her life.

She looked back on her two selves meeting, child and woman, the bones rattled. This was the woman emerging, saying goodbye to the child, looking over the great gulf of her marriage to that other self, feeling pain at her lost childhood. Her life was beginning to take on a value in her own mind that she had never before accorded it.

She asked Jeremy to play on his flute. She looked through the window at white-winged egrets flying against the blue mountain. Would she ever know a mountain as intimately as she had known this one, she had seen it in sunset and sunrise, cloud and sun, had climbed it so many times. Closer to the house, the river cliff rose dark grey beyond the huge poplars under which she and Jeremy had played, each in a different childhood. It was over. There was no going back.

She had come closer to tears at that moment than at any other time. At home, dry-eyed though frightened, she packed up, emptied cupboards, organised the removals. She knew clearly what she was losing, feared the blankness of the time ahead, yet the inevitability of her actions seemed mirrored in all the events of that time. The destruction of their home, begun at Stephen's death, continued. It was clear that her leaving had been a flight from death and yet it was itself a death. She was leaving the past, both her own and Stephen's, and stepping into a future which would be different from anything she had ever known. Pain, oh yes, there was pain. Nothing was easy.

Jean, searching again for the right image, fitting and rejecting the pieces, fumbling through confusions, prepared for her own blindness, her own sentimentality, wanting to cut through all this to find that truth which would set her free, found herself thinking of that time as if she were a diver who remembers how, when he has spent too long underwater, he breaks the surface with a painful gasp. A child must know that moment too in her first breath of air, which is also a cry. She felt suddenly an overwhelming surge of gratitude to those who had let her go. For she knew that each time she had moved away from the life to which she had been bred, the anger of the community grew. The more they pushed her away from them, away from safety, said openly that her widowhood was a disgrace to Stephen, the closer she came to that primal shout. She was not the only one who had seen herself as the caretaker and guardian of Stephen's property and now she was being condemned for dereliction of duty. Perhaps that is why in some countries widows are encouraged to burn themselves on the corpses of their husbands. Being themselves so long possessions, part of the furniture of a man's life, it is no wonder that when faced with the responsibility of wealth, they endanger that wealth. They cannot forget those who have been made hungry by the flux of the rich. Allowed to live without husbands, they are free to question the very foundations of society. Nothing is sacred to the outsider.

Looking at herself from this distance, she no longer felt pain when she remembered uneasy evenings in comfortable sitting rooms where her married friends had entertained her. She could see herself, alone, facing them from an overstuffed armchair, while they arranged themselves before her in family groups, the parents festooned with dogs and children. They were, she now realised, marshalling the forces of their homes against her. At the time she had felt like a waif, window-shopping on cold winter evenings, longing to be asked in to those brighly-lit interiors with their warm fires and happy, united families. She knew that a wall of glass would always stand between her and their domestic scene, but she did not understand how her longing to share their love undermined their smiling patronage and turned their friendship into deadly battle.

Beginning for the first time to rattle the bones with joy, she thanked all those friends who had hated her absolutism. Had they been kinder, had they found her a place where her confusions could have been contained, where she and Jeremy would feel less lonely, she might have been tempted to dismiss her ideas as personal arrogance and settle for what nurturance the community provided. But there was nothing soft about this community. It had not reached the level of racial cruelty on which it was built by being kind and it was certainly not able to transcend itself by being kind to her. She had after all been daily reminded that she did not suffer alone. Her chronicle continued, sometimes pulled, sometimes pushed, sometimes taking a few blind steps of her own, she moved away.

'Jean, do you live *here*?' Suzie's voice cut into her life. The black theatre group were her guests as she had been theirs, yet now, visiting her, they were seeing her in relation to her home, a white woman in a social frame, and they taunted her deliberately. They turned up her record player, the noise of music blaring out over the quiet suburban lawns, they teased Jeremy about his membership of the ruling class. Yet they were her friends, closer to her than the words they spoke, compromising themselves even by their friendship with her. John sat in her kitchen, his hand round the brandy bottle, his way lost in the early hours of the morning, 'Jean, why did we come?' Their friendship had brought them, yet that friendship was something they could not afford; because she was white, they needed to go their own way without her. Paradoxically they gave her life integrity while at the same time hurting her with their rejection of her offer of comradeship. Yet unlike the community to which she belonged, they gave her support. Because they too were set on a road which they already knew would lead to suffering, and certainly was no easy way, they reached momentarily towards her; 'It's all right,' said Zac as he held her when they said goodbye, 'You will leave here, it will soon be over.'

She heard the knock through veils of sleep and knew what it was even before she got up to answer it. This had never happened before, yet she knew it, that early morning knock, heard down the ages, symbol of tyranny through fear. She leaned out of the upstairs window. At the door stood four men, only one in police uniform, they said they had a warrant to search her house. When she opened the door, they thrust a paper into her hand, but the typewritten words made no sense. Jeremy was up too, standing with her as she walked with them into the gracious sitting room.

Like the thieves they opened drawers, spilling out their contents in untidy efficiency, leaving her to pack up after them. She hovered beside them, apologetic, explaining her life. Those photographs of the African township were for an exhibition in the Cathedral, had already been shown publicly, were quite legal. Without a word they moved impassively away and up the stairs into her bedroom. Her bed was rumpled, her clothes scattered as she had removed them sleepily the night before, the privacy of her life was being invaded by those official eyes. Her panties lay on the floor, the last garment she had kicked off before jumping into bed. The uniformed officer looked at them with an expression of disgust. Must she apologise for her sex as well? She could still see them now, locked in her memory, her soiled panties, the curl of his lip. Her mind clicked shut like a guillotine.

It was enough. She would be their accomplice no longer. She refused to be a witness to their judgement of her. She would do her own judging. She left them, Jeremy stayed at their request. Accompanied by one policeman, she made herself cup after cup of coffee in the kitchen, never offering him any, showing no sign that he was there. He stood reading her gay kitchen noticeboard, sighing, moving from one leg to the other. Older than the rest, he seemed uneasy at the discourtesy of their visit, he sighed, 'Mrs Craig...' he began, in a sentence heavy with apology. She cut him short with a glance, moved away into her own silence.

Eventually it was over; she and Jeremy drank coffee and read the Sunday papers before anyone else in the street had stirred. They could not go back to bed. The house felt defiled. Four men had been able to enter their home, unlock cupboards, empty out each drawer, touch anything they liked, read the titles on the hundreds of books which Stephen had so carefully collected. The house seemed smaller, less safe, even less of a place to feel at peace. Much later Jeremy told her that he had never again slept soundly on a Saturday night. If they were to look for a haven, they had not found it here. This was no safe place. She knew that pollution was everywhere, in the ground they walked on, the air they breathed, the love they offered each other. 'Hurry,' she cried to her other self, throwing the bones, suddenly afraid that she would not be able to escape. 'Hurry, there is so much ahead, and you may die there, you could die there. Hurry! Hurry!'

She could see herself; a small figure standing in the wind on a huge sand-dune gazing out to sea. The oil-tankers looked like toy ships on the horizon. She could see how her body was becoming crumpled from the pain, how the deepening lines on her pale face showed anxiety, anger, loneliness. On that vast beach, she found her loneliness more bearable. This huge primeval space was indifferent to her presence. No rock or bird seemed to mind that she was there. It was acceptance of a kind.

It was the third winter after Stephen's death that she finally broke away. In spite of the cold nights, the days were windless, the sun, shining from a clear sky, warmed up white walls and the thick, matted grass. She sat in the garden, the contents of the cellar spread out around her on the lawn; old magazines, garden tools, broken tricycles, a child's blackboard, two lawn-mowers, boxes of old 78 records, a trunk full of documents and letters, old clothes in suitcases, a stretcher, even a commode. These were things they had not been able to cram into the house, yet had thought might some day come in useful, or that were part of a past they had not wanted to throw away. It was natural that she should start here when clearing out the house.

She was thorough, she scrutinised each object with only one criterion in mind; everything that had belonged to Stephen would be stored, what had belonged to her would be thrown away. She would not take responsibility for destroying any except her own possessions, yet her rebellion said that it would not be she who would come back for Stephen's things. She knew that when she had clung to the security which these possessions had given her, she had shut away her deepest emotions.

Squinting into the sunlight, she read through old letters, letters written to Stephen by herself, by someone called Jean, who had an untidy, breathless style, who was persistently cheerful, who assumed a bland understanding of the world. She felt totally separate from this person, preferring Stephen's tortuous romantic style to this letter-writer's trivia. Was this person really herself? She felt a rush of pity for this frightened, childish girl, and an anger, even as she tore up her own letters, keeping his, for Stephen's poor understanding of his relationship with her, his unconscious oppression of a mind which he never saw as separate from his own. Or even had much respect for. Had he? Was she being unfair? Anger, and guilt at this anger, boiled under her efficient exterior, the hands ever busy sorting, destroying, and always in such a way that she could be sure it was only herself she was erasing. Why did she do this? What instinct for self-destruction, what desire for a fresh start, what revulsion from a self who had been so pale, so without definition, content to allow another to guide her, judge her? Certainly this destruction of herself, coupled as it was with a scrupulous attention to each small object that had belonged to Stephen, was an act of aggression against him. She gave him his definition of himself, guarded it conscientiously, but she used the anger that she suddenly felt to wipe out all traces of the self who had lived so long in his shadow. Deliberately setting herself up, and for the first time, as neither daughter, wife or even mother, she cut off all links with the past, determined to carry nothing with her into her new life. She would this time make sure that what emerged was Jean, if there was anything there at all.

Looking at herself from a distance, Jean was amazed to recognise the anger. Even the scrupulous way she had fulfilled her obligations as caretaker, ensuring that she would not, could not be reproached for lack of respect for Stephen's memory, even this was part of the anger that ripped up letter after letter in her own childish scrawl.

Yes, her every action was an accusation. She was stripping herself of her past, negating seventeen years of marriage, was saying in effect that the Jean who had lived through that was not worth keeping, that she had been deluded, misunderstood, maimed. Was there self-pity in her anger? It was difficult to assess that. But how could she accuse Stephen? If there was guilt it was shared equally between them. Besides it was part of a pattern of life that she herself had only recognised when she no longer belonged to it. She had suddenly found herself out in the open, it was cold and lonely, but she was beginning to smell the scent of freedom on the wind. Her anger gave her the strength to cleanse herself, so that she could start her journey alone.

Musing over the bones, Jean remembered again that small wind-battered room in the resettlement camp, where she had not mourned, sister with sister. Although she had understood that pain and loneliness, sharing it, she had been held back by a weight of custom that had seemed to her obligatory. At last she was making her own rules. The child sitting alone in the dry river bed had never dreamed that she had a right to make demands on the world she lived in, and when she had grown up she had taken it for granted that her life would have no purpose of its own, that it waited to be transformed by the love of a man, whom she would then serve and follow in all things. She smiled, nothing works out exactly as we dream it, yet it was nevertheless true that she had believed this myth implicitly; it was as inevitable a truth to her as the sun rising or the turn of the seasons.

And it was certainly a great anger which had made her challenge her different identities, and claim a life of her own. Yet it was also true, she now saw, looking dispassionately at herself, not living each raw moment in blind experience, but standing back and seeing herself as from another world, that her sex wove a pattern through her life, linking all her separate selves together. Through her womanhood her life made sense;

hers was not an isolated anguish. She had been nurtured to accept her place without rebellion. Throughout the world women were taught like her to serve and suffer. Although she was still alone, she was at least breaking free from the mould which had kept her from reaching out to those who suffered as she did.

The house was up for sale. As she pored over the pile of stored and broken objects, a woman buyer stood on the veranda above. She knew, having walked over the house, how much work there was to do, how each cupboard and bookshelf would be crammed with forgotten treasures, each one with its own dilemma, each one demanding a different solution. 'You will never manage to finish!' joked the spectator sympathetically. It took Jean three months. It was three months of dying.

She sold nothing which was his, kept nothing which was hers. Her life had shipwrecked on Stephen's death. Now she gathered those things which were his and stored them with friends. She would no longer stand in front of a house, crammed full with possessions, to defend it from the hungry and homeless. She had left empty-handed, with nothing but these bones to put against the future. It was no wonder that they haunted her.

When she had packed up everything and moved all the furniture out, she cleaned the rooms meticulously, washing down the paintwork and the walls. Because there was no bed to sleep in, she lived for the last week with friends, returning each day to the house. The time came to say goodbye.

It was a still, warm winter's morning. Unimpeded by furniture or curtains, the sun shone in the rooms like a benediction. Unlike other empty houses that she had walked through, damp, grey houses with torn wallpaper and dirty cellars, this house was like a huge air-filled bubble, the golden floors and white walls smiled at her. She sat on the lawn in the sun, the house rising behind her, the garden spread out before her. This was her last moment as Mrs Jean Craig. For both her and the house the future was uncertain. They had shared joy and now parted.

She had barely survived. The seeker looked at her with pity.

Jean was exhausted, her clothes hung over her thin body, her skin was dry and scaly. It had been a long journey from that first death to this other death. Then she had needed all the remnants of Stephen's life to affirm her existence. Now they stood in her way. The bones she was holding were divested of flesh, smooth and well-worn by her own hands. Her hands, which had begun by holding on, had learned to throw away and were coming to terms with their own emptiness, linking her instead to a world of people she had at that time never met. The bitterness of these memories was all that held her back. She must learn to thrown the bones away as well.

Stephanie Smolensky

I told you when we started this relationship
what to expect

... I've got this very bad problem.
You see
I can't feel anything
oh except
maybe down there from time to time.

I had a pretty ropy adolescence —
I had you know this really oppressive demanding
*   mother*
I had acne; I wanked all the time;
I was scared of girls, no confidence ...
(no you really don't have to reassure me
I haven't worried about that sort of thing
for years)
anyway
I had a kind of nervous breakdown
when I was eighteen ...

— and since then?
well, ups and down you know, like everyone else —

except, once or twice (no don't ask me about it I
don't want to be more specific)
I actually got hurt
(no don't put your arm round me, I'm fine now
nobody can hurt me now
you can't, for one)

But I do want some understanding
sometimes I get a bit
well, down —
but you're not to take advantage, play any silly
games ...

on those days, I might like to go to bed a bit earlier
and stay a bit later the next morning
but you won't actually remind me about it
afterwards
if you're wise ...

Anyway, I got sidetracked —
the main point is
don't expect too much in the way of feelings. That's
how I am
We can sleep together from time to time
Whenever I want to

and talking —
yes of course we'll talk
interesting talks about things like
your poetry and my work
and yes gossip about friends

and we'll do interesting things too —
When I'm free, and not too tired.

we can eat out sometimes
            where they have
Candles, chrysanths and soy sauce bottles
on the tables —
and go to late night films and meet
our other friends shivering in the queue
                    even turn up at
the odd meeting together
            walks perhaps
                    parties ...
if your behaviour's not too primitive ...

... sex with other people? Well, of course!
Look, you're quite free —
I do not go in for
petty-bourgeois couple restrictions ... I mean
isn't that what I've just been saying?

Sometimes you surprise me you know
for a feminist you have some really weird ideas ...

And that reminds me:
Independence. I'll tell you straight.
I'm not into women
who don't lead their own lives
strongly, from their own centre.
I want someone who's got no fears about being
    alone —
(What do you mean, I'm here now and have been
the last few nights? Well? Well ... you can explain
    that one later.)
I want you to be independent
and available (within reason of course
you'll have to do other things from time to time).

...What the fuck do you mean, contradictory?
I'm perfectly reasonable! You must never
never let anybody dictate your life to you —
I mean
I respect your inner life,
I respect that you're different from me ...
I read your poems, don't I?

All I want is for you to do the same ...
Mutual respect.
Well, I can't do it for you,
no, that's something you've got to do by yourself.
I can only be your friend.

— What do you mean, a millstone?
Me? I run a fucking creche two days a week —
I practically founded the Men's Group round here,
I've been into women's problems for years.
— No, I don't find that funny, are you drunk?
Well stop laughing then. What was that?
I make up the rules?
You're fucking jealous, that's your trouble,
and hysterical and insecure,
colonising, possessive —

No, no that would be stupid. No, look ...
You're not being at all reasonable ...
Listen, why don't I put the kettle on? Eh?

... Oh and, er
look there's just one thing I did want to ask
— er, about ... um ... coming, are you ...
Well, is it ... um ... just difficult with me
Or do you actually ... have orgasms
with other people? I mean, more easily ...

Well, it's not pleasant for a man, is it
to have to ask.

Oh.

Well, I'll just make the tea.

Gillian Allnutt

An Ambivalent Situation

She met him on a train going to New York City.

'Let's go to the bar,' he said. 'Then we can smoke.'

So they sat in the bar carriage, backs to the blue-tinted double-glazed windows that distorted the world by the railroad tracks, and exchanged cigarettes and the ready-made facts of their lives, the small change that lives in coat pockets and is easily got rid of. They bought beer.

'And where are you going to stay?' he asked.

'With a friend. She's not there at the moment, but I hope there is someone in the apartment.'

'Better call them from Grand Central Station. If there's nobody home you could leave your stuff in my place.'

Ruth was afraid of New York City because she had never been there and had no way of knowing the truth of the stories she'd heard back home in London. With her rucksack it would be harder to run from the rapist. And the thought of herself in the grid of that dangerous city, herself in the streets with no certain address to be going to, was frightening.

He seemed rather stupid and wanted to talk about drugs,

but he had studied the law at Harvard. So she said OK and at Grand Central Station put a dime in the phone and got no reply from her friend's apartment, took his key and boarded the crowded subway train he pushed her into just before the doors closed.

'Broadway Local One,' he yelled and the name of the station to change at.

She changed trains, glad to get out of the crowded rackety express that hurtled along between blue-painted steel girders and felt as if it would not stop ever, even if it tried.

She stepped into the local train and found a space on one of the seats that ran down the sides of the carriage. She saw faces from all parts of the world, some closed, some staring aggressively, all tired looking.

She emerged from the subway into the hot streets and found her direction and arrived at the dark doorway of the big brownstone house on Riverside Drive where he was living that summer.

She went up the stairs and had trouble with the lock, as he'd said she would. Finally the door opened onto the living room. She looked around, creeping from room to room of the dark stuffy apartment. Three rooms: he had told her that two Texans were renting the place with him. Three men. She looked doubtfully at the narrow strip of carpet between table and fireplace in the living room. It would be uncomfortable to sleep there and she would be in the way.

When she returned in the evening from a first apprehensive foray into the wide populous streets, he was there. He'd bought beer and was making tuna fish salad, enormous American sandwiches.

They delved further into their lives over supper.

'I was married — twice,' he told her. 'One of my ex-wives lives in Connecticut now. I see her sometimes, at weekends. To talk about the alimony.'

He looked too young to have been twice wedded, but she supposed that marriage was a briefer business in America where the laws were more flexible and perhaps more readily grasped by whoever needed to make use of them.

After eating, Ruth brought out a small plastic inhaler.

'My ear is blocked. The doctor here gave me this to clear it.' She inserted the inhaler in her right nostril and sniffed long and loud.

'Let me look at that,' he said, reaching for the bottle. He looked at the label and said, 'You can get high on this stuff.'

'O yes?' replied Ruth, uninterested, intent on mopping her nose.

They went to the movies, bought more beer and sat on a bench by the river to drink it. He insisted on paying. They wandered up Broadway looking in windows.

'You'd look good in that dress,' he said, pointing. 'I'd like to buy it for you.'

'No, you mustn't. You can't do that.' She got them out of the shop before he could ask the price of it. She was puzzled, and apprehensive now, for she guessed what the only return for his apparent generosity could be.

At one in the morning they bought ham and rolls in a delicatessen. Again he would not let her pay, not even half.

'You must let me share,' Ruth said, 'I want to give something too, you know.'

'What can you give me?' There was a touch of contempt in his voice. 'You know you haven't got much money.'

In the apartment they ate more sandwiches. Then Ruth took out her diary and began to record the day's events.

'Come into my room and write. It's more comfortable in there,' he said, getting up.

'No, I'm fine here. I won't be long,' replied Ruth, biting the pen, wondering how to insist that she was going to sleep on the floor by the table. 'You go to bed. It's late. I'll just lay out my sleeping bag on the floor in here.'

He walked over to his room, went in, leaving the door ajar. Five minutes later he reappeared in undershorts and a torn vest.

'Are you coming?' he asked impatiently.

'I haven't quite finished,' Ruth prevaricated. 'There's a lot to put down, you know.'

'You can't sleep in here. The other two get up very early, go off to their courses at eight o'clock in the morning,' he explained. Then he came out with it. 'Besides, it'll make me look stupid — you sleeping on the floor here.'

Ruth answered without looking at him.

'I don't want to sleep with you.' She was uncomfortable, for she knew she was not playing according to the rules of his game. She had accepted his entertainment because he had forced her to. But now she was unwilling to fulfil her part of the bargain. Irrelevant to say she had never looked at it that way; ineffective to explain that in her own country, her own city, she would do for any visitor what he had done for her without expectation of return.

'O come on, Babes,' he said, coaxingly, persuasively, walking up to the table and sitting down beside her.

Ruth curled up inside at the word 'babes'.

'No, I'd rather sleep on the floor.'

She felt him stiffen, angered by her obstinacy. He tried another tack.

'Have you inhaled any more of that stuff?'

'No,' answered Ruth. 'It isn't time yet.'

'Well, why don't you? It might make you feel better.'

'No,' she returned, taking a firm stand on the whole question of drugs. 'Why should I want to get high?' She went on writing.

He fingered the plastic inhaler, turning it round and round in his hand. Suddenly she felt something snap in him. He thrust the bottle into her face.

'Go on, take some. I said, take some. It might make you more friendly.'

Ruth laid down her pen and looked at him. Her eyes were cold and calm. She half smiled, mocking his loss of control.

'No.'

He paced up and down the room.

'Well, are you going to sleep in my room or not? Because this is getting ridiculous. I want to get some sleep tonight. I've got to work tomorrow.'

Ruth was afraid of the violence in him and knew she must make a decision.

'What you are telling me,' she said in a cool voice, 'is that either I sleep with you or I'm out on the streets tonight. Right?'

'Yes,' he said after a brief moment of surprise. 'Yes, that's right. I'll call a cab for you, if you want.' He took a step towards the telephone.

'No, it's all right, I'll stay,' said Ruth quietly. She understood that she had made it easy for him, that perhaps such a decisive move had not been necessary. But she hadn't been able to judge the degree of self-control he possessed. Violence was unpredictable. She had wanted to make the situation clear. Now she was angry but set herself to go through with it.

She closed her diary, put it away in the rucksack, pulled out her washbag and towel. All her movements were deliberate and he watched her. When she entered the bathroom he went back into his room.

In the tiny airless bathroom with the square of window that gave onto a dark shaft in the centre of the building, she decided on curiosity. She would see what he would do with her, how far he would go against her will. She would lie like a stone, be the object woman to the tip of her cold still toes.

She entered the room. He lay beneath the sheet. It was a hot night.

'I'm going to put the light out,' she said. 'Where is the switch?' He told her.

She undressed in the dark. A diffuse white light came from the street lamp outside. The lattice of ironwork over the window (to stop the thief, the rapist, from entering in the night) cast a grid of shadows across the floor. She took her time and at last lifted the sheet and lay down on her back beside him on the rumpled mattress.

At once he leaned over and his mouth was on hers, everywhere on her face. His breath was everywhere. She stopped breathing. His hand was warm and slightly damp as it felt over her body, breasts, stomach, thighs. She lay taut with her arms by her sides, her legs straight, feet slightly apart. She did nothing but lie there, her mouth unopening, all her energy concentrated in her brain, thinking cold questioning thoughts of curiosity. He grew warmer, breathed louder, masking her stillness. She escaped into fantasy — she was the stone lady of a knight on a medieval tomb in a cold cold cathedral in England. He panted like the little dog that lay beneath her feet. His hand parted her legs, fingers scrabbling at her eagerly, finding the place, finding it dry. 'Dry, dry, don't you feel me quite dry?' thought Ruth, incredulous. How could he go on in the face of such unresponsiveness? Or had all his experience been like this? She felt contempt — but was it for the other women who had slept there with him, or for him in his insensitivity, or for herself in such a position? He pushed her legs apart, clambered on top of her body, with his hand fed himself into her, pushed, panted. And then — in, out. It must have been hard going, but he came and then at once flopped down on her, heavy, flabby, inert. It was so hot. She pushed him away.

'Did you enjoy it?' he asked, stretching out beside her, flinging his arms above his head.

Ruth did not reply and after a while he began touching her breast, playing with the nipple. She turned on her side away from his hand and he pushed her onto her stomach and started to climb over her.

'No!' she exclaimed, curling into a tight ball with a sudden quickness that surprised him.

He fell back.

'I didn't want to hurt you, Babes.'

After a while he fell asleep, his breath rasping a little in his nose.

Ruth uncurled and thought of the two ex-wives. She wondered how it would have been to walk the dark streets of that great violent city all night long.

an extract from the novel by

Marit Paulsen

translated by Nan Leunbach

You, Human Being

> *In 1972 the Stockholm publishers Raben & Sjogren brought out this first novel by a former woman industrial worker. The central figures are a married couple worn down by the inhuman demands of rationalisation and piecework in the steel industry. This excerpt follows the thoughts of the woman character throughout a night shift.*

You're beginning to get tired again now. Arms hurt unbearably — how long can you keep standing like this, lifting heavy metal sheets onto the machine.

Lift, lift, in the same rhythm, the same working tempo, same muscle movements. Hour after hour, for days, months, years?

How long can your body go on? You know very well you must stand here on the same workshop floor till you're sixty-seven years old. If you can.

How long can your soul, your dream, carry on?

Can you put up with the degradation, mistrust, contempt?

With tiredness comes doubt. But right now you're still alive enough to turn your feelings into hate. It's better for you to hate. Hate against oppression, hope of a dreamland, can carry you further. Hope, belief in a better life, in any case for the children, can give you some years to be an individual.

Individual?

Isn't it presumptuous of a worker, and in addition a woman, to believe that she's an individual — maybe you even believe you're a human being?

Look around, comrade, look round the workshop. What do you see?

Big machines, lumps of steel, with small so-called living beings tightly attached to them.

A living extension of the machines.

Only that?

Look at television, read the papers; there you see many names. You're called the public, the mass, the workforce, numbers in statistics, the Swedish people.

But there's no one who calls you human being.

You feel like standing up and crying out to the whole world:

'I'm a human being, just a human being. I have only one life, let me live it. I am not a living part of a machine, I am a being with thoughts, senses, feelings, responsibilities and will — let me use them.'

Where will you put yourself, how can you make yourself heard? You should just be quiet. Quiet.

The world is full of know-alls, the kind who know everything better than you. They know much better than you what you feel and what you think. They *know* that you are a dreamer. They know your tiredness doesn't exist.

They know that you are not a human being.

Because human beings can think, but foremen and borough council careerists think for you. Human beings have feelings of responsibility — you don't. You can't even take responsibility for the speed of your own work. Human beings have feelings, your feelings always lie, they're always subjective, your feelings just need a few nerve pills. When you have nerve pills to keep awake and sleeping pills to fall asleep, then your feelings become a little more objective.

Stop thinking, you old hag.

You can't think anyway. Your strange, crazy thoughts are woven together with your feelings. You shouldn't think when you can't analyse your thoughts, distinguish between reality and your subjective experience of your own life.

Leave the work of thinking for yourself to those with a good training and a high wage. The system has you weighed and measured. You have to fit into the limits your master has set for you.

You have to keep in time with his machine, you have to stand the noise and the dust which his timetables say you can stand.

You must stand here. Just here. Always.

Here comes the foreman bellowing.

'Have you finished the order for Lillkoping? No? What the hell did you say? You've got to be finished before twelve. That's when the lorry's coming.'

'It's impossible. The Finn's really doing what she can, but she can't keep up. I'll be damned if I can be everywhere at the same time.'

He scolds and storms about contrary bitches, shameless bitches, about bitches who don't give a damn for the factory and who stay at home to clean up. The bloody factory bitches are never sick, and they never have sick children.

They laze away their time staying at home doing the cleaning.

The hell, they must have cleaning sickness. The more kids they have, the more cleaning mad they are.

Maybe it would have been a bit better for you if you'd been a man. Then you'd have had a chance to take part in the factory's training scheme. Had a chance to change jobs. You would have liked to have done repairs. But no, women are so damned well suited for monotonous work.

Advancement for a female industrial worker means moving into an office and typing with two fingers — for four, five hundred kroner less monthly pay. You pulled yourself together enormously one day a long time ago and went up to the personnel office to ask about training. There you had it confirmed what you had always guessed, that women are awful. You alternately grinned and cried over what you heard from the gorilla with the castrated soul.

Bitches are only meant to be used for what they are made for: to do a monotonous job in a screwed-up tempo.

Furthermore, the factory has no use for bitches and absolutely none for those who are snooty enough to want a qualified job. You can only be counted as good as a man if you are at least fifty percent better than he is. But you have full freedom to compete on equal conditions. Women have such bad working motivation. Yes. How the hell should it be otherwise, with eighteen hours work out of twenty-four a day. Women have too little ambition. Yes, indeed they have. They're not brought up to have other ambitions than to crochet from the pattern of the well-known lady and to bake Aunt Lydia's tarts. To nosewipe their children into slavery. To fetch clean underpants for their husbands. If any woman shows ambition — perhaps only looking after herself, or bringing in a bit of money, then suddenly she's not a woman anymore.

The machine helps you to thump out the oaths.

Just now the machine is the only thing you don't hate with your whole heart.

That those men are not ashamed of themselves, those men who like to live it up on the extra money the wives bring in, but who won't lift a finger to help at home.

Isn't it like pimping, when he lives from what her body can drag in?

Not even to look after the kids so she can go to the union meeting, try and find a clever spokesman.

The union, yes, that hasn't any use for women either, for bitches.

Maybe for making coffee?

Now and again you've had to listen to what you're worth, even there.

'Women are made to go to bed with, but not bloody well to negotiate with.' For all that, stupid people are everywhere, even in the union movement itself.

Thoughts buzz on in time with the machine.

Dear machine, you are certainly the only one who understands how damned hopeless everything is. You also stand bolted fast in this hell. You also get more and more worn out, battered and defective. But you have a few advantages over your keeper. If there's any trouble with you, the factory sees to it that you have a whole mass of machine doctors. Your thoughts come and go.

You, mother, who are away from your kids eight hours in twenty-four, you who neglect them, you who don't give a damn about the happiness of your children, you who are always sour, peevish and tired. Exactly, *you* shouldn't have to run to meetings on the evenings when you could be at home with your kids.

No, you factory worker bitch, however you twist and turn, you can never break your vicious circle.

Whatever you do, however you do it, you'll be wrong. You should have stayed at home. You should have used your life to gossip, put rollers in your hair, put on eyeshadow, bake fancy buns.

You should have forced your husband to do extra work. You should have brought up your children to slavery.

Then you'd have been a real woman, then you'd have been a normal human being.

You shouldn't care a damn about stupid things, like supporting yourself, grown-up human being, you shouldn't take on things like trying to improve conditions.

You should leave the job of improving the world to men, preferably those apes with high qualifications and wages.

So tiredness has crushed you once again. Cold shivers of tiredness and feelings of fear tear your soul to shreds, once more. Can you ever collect them again? Will you see your dreamland one more time? At last, one more shift has come to an end. It's wonderful to get clothes, oil, dust and sweat off.

Then you jog home again, cold fever comes creeping back again, back aches.

Now you'll get a rest, for two hours and thirty minutes.

After that there's a new day, a new shift — the home shift.

You go home to bed, you who believe so much, who all the same are not allowed to believe. You go home to bed, you who are so much, but who all the same are nothing.

You are a woman, worker, employed, mother, low paid, extra, production factor, spouse, consumer.

Angela Hamblin

Sensitivity

He always had
a special kind of feeling
for the countryside
it's my kind of
intensity, he said.
Every year on our
annual holiday
he would take me
to look at
hillsides
hedgerows
open fields or
winding valleys
and tell me
of their
beauty.

Once on a Scottish hillside
he braved the cold

March wind to
climb yet further
and show me the view
from beyond the
next ridge

But the early Scottish dusk
was already upon us
and the cold bit deep
into my body and
all i could think of
was the child
i carried in my womb
and the legs
(weary now after six
months pregnancy)
that refused to
carry me further

And i feared that
i would die
out here
on this lonely
Scottish hillside
like some wind-lashed
defeated animal
who knowing that
she can't go on
lies down
and prepares
for death

And he couldn't understand
my anger
and helpless rage
couldn't comprehend
my refusal to be

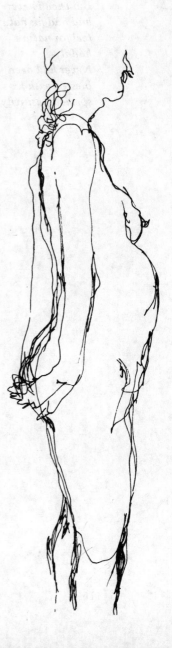

moved by the beauty
set out before me.
But then i never
had had his natural
feel for nature
had i?
Never had been
blessed with his
special sensitivity.

Fay Weldon

Pearly Oats

'Pearly Porage Oats — a nourishing way to start the day' had done the public very well for sixty years, but clearly would do no longer. The client, lethargic for so long but now prodded by falling sales and the onslaught of muesli onto the nation's breakfast tables, rumbled and heaved and demanded a different slogan; something newer and better: something more emotional, probably to do with mother love.

The task of shaping the new campaign went, appropriately enough, to Audrey Camelot. A bright name for a bright girl, as the Accounts Executive said. Audrey, he told the client, could pull the loving evocations of family life out of thin air, as could no one else, and twine them with commercial brightness, and impart her enthusiasms to art director and marketing man, and nimbly come up trumps, time and time again, with a campaign which not only sold well on account of its creativity, rationality and sensitivity, but demanded the professional respect of clients and advertisers everywhere. So he said, handsome, golden man that he was.

Audrey, for some reason, had trouble with Pearly Oats.

*Pearly Porage, perfect Porage,
fattening way to an old-fashioned day?*

A wild and wandering mind has its usefulness in advertising, but not when it appears to hate the product it is required to dwell upon. Nothing wrong with the product — no more nor less than a nourishing way to start the day, as everyone in the country knew, and had for decades. Something wrong with Audrey, perhaps? Or so the Accounts Executive wondered.

Of course, said Audrey snappily to the Accounts Executive, there's something wrong with me, there's something wrong with all of us, but where does that get us? So long as it gets us somewhere by the end of the week, he replied, and Audrey stretched her arms behind her back, absently and automatically, so that her breasts showed to advantage. The Accounts Executive knew them well, as it happened, but familiarity never dulled his fondness for them.

'You always get like this just before you come up with something,' he reassured her, father to his little girl, and she hoped so, and left with a cheerful skip and a hop, and a bounce of delectable bosom, warming his heart.

To business then. 'Early Pearly? Swirly Pearly on the plate, early pearly by the gate?'

Something there, but where was the mother love? There clearly had to be mother love. The client, eldest son of the first founder of Pearly Porage Oats, had recently re-married and his new young wife was pregnant. The day-to-day practicalities of breakfast would hardly entrance him: that might come later, but not now. He would see breakfast as something to linger over, not merely to get through in order to get to the school bus. Tuesday, Wednesday, Thursday passed. Friday morning.

At midday on Friday the telephone rang. Daisy Duncan, Audrey's friend. They'd been to the same Council school, back-of-the-buildings in a London slum. It was demolished now, but its memory still lived. A group of hopeful, lively children, fighting their way to a better life. Great things had been promised for Audrey, and greater still for Daisy, whose poems had appeared for three years running in a Poetry in British Schools' publication. Daisy could embroider, too, and reached Grade 8 on the piano. A plain girl with a large nose and a muddy complexion, but lively and creative, with a host of friends. Pretty, lonelier Audrey merely passed exams: Daisy had real talent.

But now Daisy was in tears, and Audrey seldom cried. At 12.10 Audrey left the office, took a taxi and went to visit Daisy.

'I used to think,' said Daisy sadly, that everything would get better when I got to be forty. I was forty yesterday and it hasn't.' 'I would have sent you a card,' said Audrey, 'only I thought you might prefer to forget.'

Daisy on the sofa, still in her nightie, her narrow, plain face swollen with tears, her knobbly toes poking out from beneath a quilt, too distressed, apparently, to so much as get up and do the obvious tasks — sweeping the table free of crumbs, clearing the grease from the sink.

Well, someone has to do them. Daisy's friend Audrey took up dustpan and dishcloth in her well-manicured hands, and saw to it all, careful not to spot her denim Yves St Laurent skirt and jacket, or mark her yellow calf shoes.

'You just forgot,' said Daisy mournfully. 'But it's good of you to come. I thought you'd be having some smart lunch in some expense account restaurant. You are lucky.' 'They all taste alike,' said Audrey, lightly, lying.

Audrey had come at once, forswearing the excitement of lunch at Simpson's — a little too much Campari before the meal, then perhaps an avocado vinaigrette, then a plate of thinly cut rare beef, with a green salad, and a good claret, and black coffee — with an accounts director who was trying to get her to bed. Audrey was always gratified and excited when some grey-suited man or other actually, and as a long-term project, and in an old-fashioned way, set about seducing her. Little me, little Audrey! It happened only rarely, of course, these days; not because Audrey's face or figure betrayed her age or because her sexual attractiveness had in any way diminished — on the contrary — but because the world had changed about her;

119

sexual transactions had become a simple, quicker, cheaper matter of will you, won't you, no harm done either way, no money spent, and the main obstacle to union being opportunity, not readiness.

Mind you, Audrey's advertising agency, as she was well aware, was inhabited by golden people, who had the confidence of their looks, youth and intelligence, and who did not suffer, as the rest of the world still seemed to, the fear of personal humiliation and sexual rejection.

But what happened to them when they got old? Were they fired, did they resign, was there some other advertising agency somewhere, especially designed for oldsters, located somewhere in the sticks, where they all, the tarnished men and women, went? No one stepped into the gilded agency lift of a morning, or out of it of an evening, who was not healthy, handsome, youthful and able. Only the personnel officer, strangely, limped and was old, old: old so far beyond sex, so far the other side of pensionable age, as to hardly count as human.

Audrey, creaming her face night and morning with a lotion well imbued with revitalising essence, would sometimes worry about these things, but not for long. The night ahead, the day in front, was too busy, too full of challenges, too stuffed with the admiration of the opposite sex and that of her professional colleagues, to allow any real anxiety the time it needed to clutch her heart properly and make her catch her breath with fear.

The Pearly Porage Way to eternal life, eternal youth? Oh, come along now Audrey, enough of this fantasy; where's the mother love?

Audrey's husband Jordan had gone off long ago, long ago. 'I did warn you,' Daisy had said then, sobbing bitterly on her friend's behalf, speaking with all the wisdom of the early sixties, 'you can't hold down a marriage *and* a career. Not fair to a husband, not fair to the children. Now see what's happened! I told you so! Oh, Audrey, poor Audrey!'

Daisy, with her three little ones at her heels, clamouring and clamourous, secure in the knowledge that her way was the best, that the sacrifice of self would be rewarded in the end.

After the divorce Jordan took Audrey's two, boy and girl, pigeon pair, off to the States supposedly on holiday, but never returned them. Audrey had fought a little, not too much. Glad, in the end, to be finally rid of him, and them: free to work, to drink after hours, to bed whom she pleased, as long as she pleased, without guilt or the pervasive sense of hurry that seemed to go with motherhood. She could always tell, in the gilt-panelled agency lift, who were the mothers, and who weren't. Mothers had chipped nail varnish and harassed eyes. No time!

There might be some ideal world, somewhere, thought Audrey, where docile children did smile up at mothers from cosy cots: where husbands considered their wives' thoughts, feelings and ambitions as important as their own; where housekeepers actually kept house for working mothers; and Pearly Porage Oats poured endlessly from a pan which never needed cleaning. She certainly wished it existed. If writing about it would only make it so! This honeyed world of home and polished furniture and soft looks, where men were still men and women still women! She did not deceive her readers — (if advertisements can be said to be read) no, Audrey offered them her dreams, in all sincerity. And they accepted them, as dreams: and bought, as talismans.

And now here's poor Daisy, in tears these days for herself, and not for her friend.

Audrey's mind flickered on, as she mixed Daisy some reviving whisky and water in a smudged glass. Pearly Porage Oats. Powerful Porage Oats. Getting warmer, Audrey! Warmth, that's it. A plate of Pearly Porage, warmer than a mother's love. No. Too crude, and anyway the Advertising Standards Authority wouldn't have it. Nothing could be warmer than a mother's love, they'd say. Nothing. Why then; Pearly Porage, just as warm as mother's love. Loving mother, warming day! Prove your love, with warming Pearly Porage Oats. The trouble being, pearls are cold but Porage is hot. Iced Pearly Porage Oats — the midsummer breakfast for midnight people! Come on now, Audrey! Please!

'It's not like you to let the house go, Daisy,' chided Audrey. 'It's his house, not mine,' hissed Daisy, 'he makes that clear enough. Why should I bother to clean it. Let her do it.'

Her parents should never have called her Daisy, Audrey had always thought it, inflicting upon their daughter a chirpy, peeping sweetness, which the skinny, wilful Daisy could never properly incorporate into herself. Their ambition for her. 'Donald says I've got to move out so he can live in comfort with his paramour and her brats, and I'll have to make do with a pokey flat somewhere.' 'But Daisy,' said Audrey, 'you've been living here with his so-called paramour's husband for six months. He was bound to object.'

'It's altogether different. You must see it's different.'

But Audrey could not bring herself to see. She could not, on this occasion, even for Daisy's sake, be bothered to remember the details of the particular mess of this particular marriage, which was like yet so unlike all the other messes the neurotic married everywhere manage to make of their lives: could not be bothered to register the small print, the tales of coincidence, lust overheard, letters intercepted, messages misunderstood, the general crossing of wires, which accompany the dawning of illicit love and the ending of married love, and which in fiction appear improbable to the point of indignity, and in real life come two a penny: but which are all sure to end in tears, bitterness, and the wrecked lives of confused children. And all for what? The gratification of the flesh?

Dodge when you see a coincidence coming. It will end in no good. If you meet an ex-lover by amazing chance, a missed train, a crossed line, cut him dead, walk quietly past. Fate is against you, not for you, and signalling as much.

Audrey sleeps with married men: brief interludes, happy memories: should life be more than this? Daisy committed adultery — she uses the extraordinary term herself — just once, with a married man, confessed, and before she knew where she was her psychiatrist husband Donald (A doctor! Oh Daisy, what a catch! Out of the working classes, at last; socially mobile: we

122

knew you'd do it, we little girls at the Council school!) was sleeping with her lover's wife, Dora by name, and going to live with her moreover; and her own lover, of that one, single occasion, unable to return home, but obliged to come to live with Daisy, for the sake of a bed. Well, so she said — and the seven children of both marriages shuttling between the two households. Daisy's three, nearly full grown, left home in consequence a mite too early for their own good: but her rival Dora's four were very young: had to have nappies changed and bottles made up. Poor Daisy. Her lover left eventually for younger blood, but still his four were dumped on her, of a weekend, so Donald and Dora could copulate in peace. And now Donald wanted his home back, the better to house his new lady and the four young children.

After all, Daisy started it. Donald could never forgive her for breaking up his home in the way she had. And had he not paid for the house, after all, working for it all these years, while Daisy sat back and scribbled the occasional poem, and filled the house up with queers and young musicians he couldn't get on with and clearly cuckolded him regularly. Who was to believe Daisy when she said but it was only the once, the one man, the one time, I was drunk? Who wanted to believe her? Who ever believes the pregnant young girl who cries, but it was the first time! Only once and only him. Never before and never after. Life's not like that.

Oh, but it is. Richer, wilder and stranger than fiction, by far.

> *Pearly Oats, the way to a child's heart.*
> *Mother power, porage power. Pearly Porage Power.*
> *The Pearl at the heart of breakfast.*

Daisy sobbed: the sound broke into Audrey's train of thought. Real life must come before advertising, she told herself. What's happening to me?

'Perhaps you'd better have a tranquiliser,' said Audrey, doubtfully.

Indignation stopped Daisy's tears.

'Throughout my married life,' said Daisy, 'as you ought to know, Audrey, whenever I seemed depressed or reproachful, Donald would hand me pills. Stand over me until I took them. I spent most of my life in a stupor. Whatever the latest thing was that they handed out in the acute wards, to keep up the latest myth, enable them to say they'd thrown away the keys of the loony bins — those were the pills he'd dole out to me. Experimenting, no doubt, in the ways of best achieving a quiet life. And look what he did to the children.'

That Audrey could remember. Donald started Debbie on tranquilisers when she complained of nightmares at the age of three, and she was found to be still on them at the age of nine, when a teacher enquired why the child spent her days in school sleeping.

'But why did you go on giving them?' Audrey had enquired of Daisy, horrified. 'Because I didn't know what they were, and he was a doctor,' pleaded Daisy. 'I thought he knew best.'

Donald treated David with hormones to speed up a delayed puberty, to the detriment of his personality. Or such was the probation officer's defence when David was presently in trouble with the police, peddling drugs, stealing cigarettes. Donald gave Doreen aversion therapy to cure a mild attack of teenage homosexuality, thus fixing the tendency for life. Or so Daisy said.

My own children, though Audrey, where are they now? Wholesome young Americans, sixteen and seventeen, freckled and free. I hope. Thank God I don't have responsibility for them. Why do some people's lives go sour?

Mother flown? Pearly Porage Oats, the perfect mother surrogate! Why bother with mother when P-Porage will do?

Daisy consented to get up off the sofa and dress. Something achieved! 'Of course, my parents have cast me off,' said Daisy. 'The world can't abide an abandoned wife.' 'But Daisy, you did abandon Donald first.' Useless.

Audrey's father died when she was six, her mother when she was twelve. What better gift can a mother give a daughter than to die early? So the daughter can endure her own life, unobserved; go to hell with no one grieving.

'I haven't been asked out anywhere since Donald left.'

Delightful Daisy, whom everyone loved — funny, witty and brave, popular everywhere: dragging the tatters of her life behind, like some once luxurious gown caught up in a carriage wheel, mangled but still amazing: Daisy, sheltered in those days by the looming shadow of a husband. No need for his presence in the flesh: the thought of him would do, make Daisy safe. Now he's gone, and Daisy's naked in her distress, and it might be catching. Probably is.

Pearls before swine, porage before bacon. They need a 2-course breakfast! No. Not Nutrition. Mother love. Please! Pearly smiles, early smiles. Warming the cockles of a mother's heart. Cockles? Oysters, surely. Pearls. Or mussels. Oh, Audrey!

Muesli and the top of the milk for Audrey's passing strangers. Fresh coffee and hot milk if they're lucky, but mostly cold. The flesh languid, the spirit soothed, but the mind looking forward to the closing of the front door, the return of privacy. No, don't ring me, I'll ring you. Audrey, taking her pleasures where she finds them, careful they don't change to pain.

'Christ,' said Audrey aloud, startling Daisy, 'where will it all end?' 'Death,' said Daisy, her face wiped, her waist belted, life returning, pleasure starting up in her again — this her great charm, her great strength; her resilience, the way she loved, even in her distress, to bandy words, phrases, friendship, gossip. 'That's where it will all end. In the long run we're all dead. It's the short run interests me. If only I had a party to go to. Perhaps I'll give one.'

Donald claimed that Daisy neglected the children, never once putting their interests before her own: and that David's delinquency, Debbie's apathy, and Doreen's gayness could all be laid firmly at Daisy's door. Told the judge, and the judge believed him.

Donald had told Audrey so, too, one night some three years ago, while they lay clasped together on the sofa in the

125

consulting room, and Audrey had half-believed him. The same shabby sofa, now in the kitchen, on which today Daisy had lain and sobbed. It had seemed at the time that Donald needed someone to talk to, rather than someone for sexual congress — the latter being of such short duration.

Audrey had called to see Daisy one evening, and found her out, but Donald advancing on her out of the dark hall, upset — so he said — because Daisy should so callously have abandoned her self-appointed role as faithful wife, happy mother, and secure friend — always at home when one called, and no need to ring, if only for the difficulty she always had finding babysitters.

'They may have their ups and downs, Donald and Daisy, but they're like that, like that!' Two fingers crossed. Everyone believed it. Side by side through life's vicissitudes. Someone had to be.

Pearly Oats! Your mother thrived on it! So did you! Now it's your children's turn.

Donald and Daisy. Other marriages came and went. Theirs was for ever.

'If Daisy's out with a married man,' said Audrey then, to Donald, lightly, 'perhaps you should take out the wife!'

Had she put the notion in Donald's head? Could one's passing words, so lightly spoken, really result in such terrible unheaval in so many lives?

Well, if they could stop the national flow from porage to muesli, no doubt they could break a marriage or so. Words are powerful things.

Before turning his attention to Dora, so much was for certain, Donald had taken advantage of Audrey's unexpected and comforting presence and copulated with her in the consulting room. Two naughty, upset children, behind mother's back. Rows and rows of pills everywhere, on shelves and cupboards and desks, to quench grief, staunch tears, stifle argument, quell resentment and reproach. Even, Audrey suspected, to increase sexual appetite, for the determination of Donald's approach was far bolder than the tentative nature of his actual performance. Daisy had always complained that Donald was semi-impotent. 'But it doesn't matter,' Audrey would say to her; 'I seem to get most turned on by men who hardly can.' But Audrey could see that as the years passed, it might well begin to matter.

Be all that as it may, no wonder Audrey now comes running whenever Daisy cries. Guilt? No, too strong a word. A sense, rather, that she failed by giving herself where it was easiest, opened her legs in the light of a lamp chosen by Daisy, her artistic friend, to Daisy's husband, in the ridiculous hope of being included in a family group, making it whole again. That had not been the way to do it.

All the goodness of the grain — the warming power of Pearly Oats.

'Daisy,' said Audrey now, 'Donald was a dead loss. For God's sake pull yourself together, get a job, take a teacher's training course. You can't fasten yourself to a man in your youth and be still clinging on with your fingernails twenty years later. It isn't natural.' 'But he's half me,' Daisy wailed. 'I hated him for years but he's still half me.' 'Nonsense. He's half Dora, now. We're all interchangeable, all dispensible. Do try and face it, Daisy.'

Early smiles and Pearly wiles.

'It was always supposed to be enough,' said Daisy bitterly, 'to be a wife and mother.' 'Wives and mothers wear out quickly,' said Audrey. 'In any case, if that's how you see yourself, you're just about past child-bearing age, and your husband doesn't want you — so you're finished. Well, so am I, in my advertising agency. I'm getting too old, too good at my work. I'm too expensive. It's a man's world. Newer, cheaper, brighter young women come along. Serve us right, the pair of us, for trying to ride the waves, buck the system, last too long.' 'What will we do?' asked Daisy, childlike. 'Come and live with me if you like,' offered Audrey, the thought coming out of nowhere. Could she bear it? Yes, probably. 'At any rate for a time,' she added, cautiously.

Tears sprang anew to Daisy's eyes.

'I don't know,' she said, gratefully, 'but I'll think about it.'

'I must get back to the office,' said Audrey. 'I'm working on a new campaign.' 'What?' 'Pearly Porage Oats.' 'We always have them,' said Daisy. 'Well, had. In the days when I cooked breakfast and we'd all sit down like a proper family.'

Proper families choose Pearly Porage Oats.

What's a proper family?

Why, you, me and the children, my love. On our good days.

'We had our good days,' said Daisy, smiling, magically, brightly, almost dancing: skinny and tired that she is; her hair now wiry, not silky, and beginning to grey; eyes weary about the lids, and having produced far too many tears since first they saw the light of day, to an extent nature can hardly have intended, overworking fragile tear ducts.

Step, two three. Step, two three. Daisy dances about the room like a young girl. 'I try to remember the good days. Don't you?'

Good family days begin with Porage Oats. Perhaps. But Porage Oats don't make good days. Keep the distinction clear! And move to muesli when you must.

When Audrey got back to the office she found confusion and distress. Pearly Porage Oats had been taken over by Active Breakfast Foods — an account also held by Audrey's agency — and there had been some necessary realignment of work, and seven people in the creative department, including Audrey, were to be made redundant. The Accounts Executive was to go; so was the lunchdate Audrey had missed on Daisy's behalf.

'Of course,' said the Accounts Executive sadly, 'it's all a question of pensions. Firms nowadays are run by accountants. One way or another they make sure they're never landed with an employee of pensionable age.'

Looking at him closely, Audrey could see beyond the gold to the wrinkles round his eyes and the greying of his hair, and observed that though his midriff was firm and strong, and his voice young and cheerful, and his phraseology constantly revised and kept up to date, that nevertheless the truth of age was breaking through; the sadness of long experience.

'Say what you like about it being a man's world, Audrey —

and I know you do — it's certainly turned into a young person's world, male or female. Still, we mustn't complain: we had our good days!'

And nor they do, and so they had.

Helen Dunmore

If no revolution come

If no revolution come
star clusters
will brush heavy on the sky

and grapes burst
into the mouths of fifteen
well-fed men,

these honest men
will build them houses like pork palaces
if no revolution come,

short-life dust children
will be crumbling in the sun —
they have to score like this
if no revolution come.

The sadness of people,
don't look at it too long:

you're studying for madness
if no revolution come.

If no revolution come
it will be born sleeping,
it will be heavy as baby
playing on mama's bones,

it will be gun-thumping on Sunday
and easy good time
for men who make money,

for men who make money
grow like a roof
so the rubbish of people
can't live underneath.

If no revolution come
star clusters
will drop heavy from the sky

and blood burst
out of the mouths of fifteen
washing women,

and the land-owners will drink us
one body by one:
they have to score like this
if no revolution come.

The Polish husband

The traffic halted
and for a moment
the broad green avenue
hung like a wave,

while a woman crossing
stopped me, and said

'Can you show me my wedding?
— in which church is it going to be held?'

The lorries were hooting at her
as she stood there on the island
for her cloak fell back
and under it her legs were bare.
Her hair was dyed blonde
and her sad face deeply tanned.

I asked her, 'What is the name of your husband?'
She wasn't sure, but she knew his first name was Joe,
she'd met him in Poland
and this was the time for the wedding.

There was a cathedral behind us
and a sign to the centre of the town
'I am not an expert on weddings'
I said, 'But take that honey-coloured building
that squats on its lawns like a cat —
at least there's music playing inside it.'

So she ran with her heels tapping
and the long, narrow folds of her cloak falling apart.
A veil on wire flew from her head,
her white figure ducked in the porch and blew out.

But Joe, the Polish man. In the rush of this town
I can't say whether she even found him
to go up the incense-heavy church beside him
under the bridal weight of her clothes,
or whether he was one of the lorry drivers
to whom her brown, hurrying legs were exposed.

Margaret Rodriguez

The Vote

The day of the Senate elections dawned grey. The parties had not been relying on sunshine to bring out the voters, it was the rainy season, but it was unusual for the sky to be overcast so early.

The men on polling station duty were already settling down behind the wooden trestle tables which had been set up on street corners, buttoned into raincoats if they owned them, wrapped in sheets of plastic if they didn't.

A large turn-out was expected, probably the largest ever, not that any upset of the status quo was anticipated, but because for the first time the Government had carried out a massive publicity campaign urging everyone over the age of eighteen to register as voters.

The most successful medium which had been used was television; even those who can't read and write can watch television. Juana Perez was one of the illiterates who had received the message, and it had registered in her mind as an act of dignity it was her duty to perform. In fact it had seldom left her mind during the closing months of the campaign. By now the thought of marking her X had been striking terror in her heart for days.

Juana was twenty-six and had been a domestic servant for thirteen years. For her, the weekly day of rest would not begin until the family had breakfasted and the two cars were cleaned. But this was a better household than many she had worked in, and it had been the Senora of the house who had taken Juana along to register when she went herself.

The Senora didn't actually expect her maid to remember to go along and vote. But alone though she might be at the moment of suffrage, Juana had no intention of forgetting.

When her duties were done she went to her room at the end of the yard to change her skirt and brush her hair. Then she left to take the second class bus out to the remote suburbs where her two children lived with her parents.

She had a boy and a girl, both by different fathers who had abandoned Juana, and so she worked in the city to support the two generations who would be anxiously expecting her now. On the bus, every nerve in Juana's body was strained with the effort of holding in her head all she had been told about the balloting procedure.

She was only vaguely aware of the purpose of the elections — to elect a new Senate — and was totally ignorant of the issues at stake. It had never occurred to her to ask herself whether the Government had provided her with a reasonable standard of living, or whether any other might give her an opportunity of a better life. She was aware only of her duty to vote. The campaign propaganda had seen to it that those who couldn't read knew that the ruling party was represented on the ballot slip by the colours of the national flag. Simple enough. Red, white and green. Juana had known that from early childhood.

When she got off the bus she walked through streets which were unusually sombre for a Sunday, but she knew this was due more to the fact that the bars were closed and the sale of alcohol prohibited than to the import of the elections.

The two children were waiting at the door, excited at the prospect of an outing, for after she had voted Juana was going to take them to the park. Inside the two room house, Juana's father was lying on the bed (there was little else to do on such a dry Sunday) and her mother, as usual, was cooking. Juana didn't linger in the house, but set off confidently through the muddy streets, ravaged by a particularly heavy rainy season, while the children ran on ahead. But as the wooden table came into view on the corner of the street her nerve failed her, and she walked straight past.

'Mama,' her seven-year-old son cried in amazement, 'I thought you were going to vote?'

'Yes, son, I am,' she replied, blushing and looking round to see whether anyone had heard him.

'But there it is — that's where you have to do it.'

There was no alternative. In her son's eyes it was all very easy, she couldn't let him down.

She turned round and walked up to the table holding each child by the hand, feeling their eyes solemnly staring at the man who was asking for her registration card.

'Here, Senora,' the man handed her a slip of paper.

What was she supposed to do with it? Her bewildered look told him everything.

'Take it to that table over there,' the man said, standing up to stretch his legs.

But what to do with it there? All previous instructions had gone out of her head. The television commercial explaining everything so carefully ... she had seen it at least fifty times, but what had it said?

If at that moment someone had asked her what the colours of the national flag were, she would not have been able to answer.

'What do I have to do with it?' she stammered, her wild eyes meeting the man's.

'Put your cross next to one of the parties, fold the paper and put it in the black box,' he replied patiently.

He was used to this type of question.

Juana stabbed at the paper with the pencil she found dangling from a piece of string. Her cross landed at the top of the paper.

136

'I put it at the top,' she almost shouted.

'Ay Senora,' the tired voice replied. 'The parties are further down on the paper. Remember,' he said speaking slowly and distinctly now as if he'd said everything a hundred times already that day. 'The PPU has the symbol of the national flag — the same colours.'

And sure enough there it was, a red, white and green circle, she remembered now, and there underneath was a blue and yellow circle, and there were two others below that. But Juana was beyond caring what the others meant, she made another cross, and with her head bowed she folded the paper and dropped it into the black box.

Nobody was taking any notice of her, the dilemma of the illiterate was a common occurrence, especially among women. Juana slunk away from the ballot box, unable to meet her son's eyes. She had expected to feel a moment of dignity, just one moment in a lifetime of humiliation, but there it was again, the familiar feeling washing over her in waves of shame.

At the end of the street she caught hold of her children's hands, and as they ran for shelter from the afternoon downpour, she silently vowed never to vote again.

Alice Walker

Her Sweet Jerome

Ties she had bought him hung on the closet door, which now swung open as she hurled herself again and again into the closet. Glorious ties, some with birds and dancing women in grass skirts painted on by hand, some with little polka dots with bigger dots dispersed among them. Some red, lots red and green, and one purple, with a golden star, through the centre of which went his gold mustang stickpin, which she had also given him. She looked in the pockets of the black leather jacket he had reluctantly worn the night before. Three of his suits, a pair of blue twill work pants, an old grey sweater with a hood and pockets lay thrown across the bed. The jacket leather was sleazy and damply clinging to her hands. She had bought it for him, as well as the three suits: one light blue with side vents, one gold with green specks, and one reddish that had a silver imitation-silk vest. The pockets of the jacket came softly outward from the lining like skinny milktoast rats. Empty. Slowly she sank down on the bed and began to knead, with blunt anxious fingers, all the pockets in all the clothes piled around her. First the blue suit, then the gold with green, then the reddish one that he said he didn't like most of all, but which he would sometimes wear if she agreed to stay home, or if she promised not to touch him anywhere at all while he was getting dressed.

She was a big awkward woman, with big bones and hard rubbery flesh. Her short arms ended in ham hands, and her neck was a squat roll of fat that protruded behind her head as a big bump. Her skin was rough and puffy, with plump molelike freckles down her cheeks. Her eyes glowered from under the mountain of her brow and were circled with expensive mauve shadow. They were nervous and quick when she was flustered and darted about at nothing in particular while she was dressing hair or talking to people.

Her troubles started noticeably when she fell in love with a studiously quiet schoolteacher, Mr Jerome Franklin Washington III, who was ten years younger than she. She told herself that she shouldn't want him, he was so little and cute and young, but when she took into account that he was a schoolteacher, well, she just couldn't seem to get any rest until, as she put it, 'I were Mr and Mrs Jerome Franklin Washington the third, *and that's the truth!*'

She owned a small beauty shop at the back of her father's funeral home, and they were known as 'coloured folks with money'. She made pretty good herself, though she didn't like standing on her feet so much, and her father let anybody know she wasn't getting any of his money while he was alive. She was proud to say she had never asked him for any. He started relenting kind of fast when he heard she planned to add a schoolteacher to the family, which consisted of funeral directors and bootleggers, but she cut him off quick and said she didn't want anybody to take care of her man but her. She had learned how to do hair from an old woman who ran a shop on the other side of town and was proud to say that she could make her own way. And much better than some. She was fond of telling schoolteachers (women schoolteachers) that she didn't miss her 'eddicashion' as much as some did who had no learning and no money both together. She had a low opinion of

139

women schoolteachers, because before and after her marriage to Jerome Franklin Washington III, they were the only females to whom he cared to talk.

The first time she saw him he was walking past the window of her shop with an armful of books and his coat thrown casually over his arm. Looking so neat and *cute*. What popped into her mind was that if he was hers the first thing she would get him was a sweet little red car to drive. And she worked and went into debt and got it for him, too — after she got *him* — but then she could tell he didn't like it much because it was only a Chevy. She had started right away to save up so she could make a downpayment on a brand-new white Buick deluxe, with automatic drive and whitewall tires.

Jerome was dapper, every inch a gentleman, as anybody with half an eye could see. That's what she told everybody before they were married. He was beating her black and blue even then, so that every time you saw her she was sporting her 'shades'. She could not open her mouth without him wincing and pretending he couldn't stand it, so he would knock her out of the room to keep her from talking to him. She tried to be sexy and stylish, and was, in her fashion, with a predominant taste for pastel taffetas and orange shoes. In the summertime she paid twenty dollars for big umbrella hats with bows and flowers on them and when she wore black and white together she would liven it up with elbow-length gloves of red satin. She was genuinely undecided when she woke up in the morning whether she really outstripped the other girls in town for beauty, but could convince herself that she was equally good-looking by the time she had breakfast on the table. She was always talking with a lot of extra movement to her thick coarse mouth, with its hair tufts at the corners, and when she drank coffee she held the cup over the saucer with her little finger sticking out, while she crossed her short hairy legs at the knees.

If her husband laughed at her high heels as she teetered and minced off to church on Sunday mornings, with her hair greased and curled and her new dress bunching up at the top of her girdle, she pretended his eyes were approving. Other times, when he didn't bother to look up from his books and only muttered curses if she tried to kiss him good-bye, she did not know whether to laugh or cry. However, her public manner was serene.

'I just don't know how some womens can stand it, honey,' she would say slowly, twisting her head to the side and upward in an elegant manner. 'One thing my husband does not do,' she would enunciate grandly, 'he don't beat me!' And she would sit back and smile in her pleased oily fat way. Usually her listeners, captive women with wet hair, would simply smile and nod in sympathy and say, looking at one another or at her black eye, 'You say he don't? Hummmm, well, hush your mouf.' And she would continue curling or massaging or straightening their hair, fixing her face in a steamy dignified mask that encouraged snickers.

It was in her shop that she first heard the giggling and saw the smirks. It was at her job that gossip gave her to understand, as one woman told her, 'Your cute little man is sticking his finger into somebody else's pie.' And she was not and could not be surprised, as she looked into the amused and self-contented face, for she had long been aware that her own pie was going — and for the longest time had been going — strictly untouched.

From that first day of slyly whispered hints, 'Your old man's puttin' something *over* on you, sweets,' she started trying to find out who he was fooling around with. Her sources of gossip were malicious and mean, but she could think of nothing else to do but believe them. She searched high and she searched low. She looked in taverns and she looked in churches. She looked in the school where he worked.

She went to whorehouses and to prayer meetings, through parks and outside the city limits, all the while buying axes and pistols and knives of all descriptions. Of course she said nothing to her sweet Jerome, who watched her manoeuvrings from behind the covers of his vast supply of paperback books. This hobby of his she heartily encouraged, relegating reading to the importance of scanning the funnies; and besides, it was something he could do at home, if she could convince him she would be completely silent for an evening, and, of course, if he would stay.

She turned the whole town upside down, looking at white girls, black women, brown beauties, ugly hags of all shades. She found nothing. And Jerome went on reading, smiling smugly as he shushed her with a carefully cleaned and lustred finger. 'Don't interrupt me,' he was always saying, and he would read some more while she stood glowering darkly behind him, muttering swears in her throaty voice, and then tramping flatfooted out of the house with her collection of weapons.

Some days she would get out of bed at four in the morning after not sleeping a wink all night, throw an old sweater around her shoulders, and begin the search. Her firm bulk became flabby. Her eyes were bloodshot and wild, her hair full of lint, nappy at the roots and greasy on the ends. She smelled bad from mouth and underarms and elsewhere. She could not sit still for a minute without jumping up in bitter vexation to run and search a house or street she thought she might have missed before.

'You been messin' with my Jerome?' she would ask whomever she caught in her quivering feverish grip. And before they had time to answer she would have them by the chin in a headlock with a long knife pressing against their necks below the ear. Such bloodchilling questioning of its residents terrified the town, especially since her madness was soon readily perceivable from her appearance. She had taken to grinding her teeth and tearing at her hair as she walked along. The townspeople, none of whom knew where she lived — or anything about her save the name of her man, 'Jerome' — were waiting for her to attempt another attack on a woman openly, or, better for them because it implied less danger to a resident, they hoped she would complete her crack-up within the confines of her own home, preferably while alone; in that event anyone seeing or hearing her would be obliged to call the authorities.

She knew this in her deranged but cunning way. But she did not let it interfere with her search. The police would never catch her, she thought; she was too clever. She had a few disguises and a thousand places to hide. A final crack-up in her own home was impossible, she reasoned contemptuously, for she did not think her husband's lover bold enough to show herself on his wife's own turf.

Meanwhile, she stopped operating the beauty shop, and her patrons were glad, for before she left for good she had had the unnerving habit of questioning a woman sitting underneath her hot comb — 'You the one ain't you?!' — and would end up burning her no matter what she said. When her father died he proudly left his money to 'the school teacher' to share or not with his wife, as he had 'learning enough to see fit'. Jerome had 'learning enough' not to give his wife one cent. The legacy pleased Jerome, though he never bought anything with the money that his wife could see. As long as the money lasted Jerome spoke of it as 'insurance'. If she asked insurance against what, he would say fire and theft. Or burglary and cyclones. When the money was gone, and it seemed to her it vanished overnight, she asked Jerome what he had bought. He said. Something very big. She said, Like what? He said, Like a tank. She did not ask any more questions after that. By that time she didn't care about the money anyhow, as long as he hadn't spent it on some woman.

As steadily as she careened downhill, Jerome advanced in the opposite direction. He was well known around town as a 'shrewd joker' and a scholar. An 'intellectual', some people called him, a word that meant nothing whatever to her. Everyone described Jerome in a different way. He had friends among the educated, whose talk she found unusually trying, not that she was ever invited to listen to any of it. His closest friend was the head of the school he taught in and had migrated south from some famous university in the North. He was a small slender man with ferociously unruly beard and large mournful eyes. He called Jerome 'brother'. The women in Jerome's group wore short kinky hair and large hoop earrings. They stuck together, calling themselves by what they termed their 'African' names, and never went to church. Along with the men, the women sometimes held 'workshops' for the young toughs of the town. She had no idea what went on in these; however, she had long since stopped believing they had anything to do with cabinetmaking or any other kind of woodwork.

Among Jerome's group of friends, or 'comrades', as he sometimes called them jokingly (or not jokingly, for all she knew), were two or three whites from the community's white college and university. Jerome didn't ordinarily like white people, and she could not understand where they fit into the group. The principal's house was the meeting place, and the whites arrived looking backward over their shoulders after nightfall. She knew, because she had watched this house night after anxious night, trying to rouse enough courage to go inside. One hot night, when a drink helped stiffen her backbone, she burst into the living room in the middle of the evening. The women, whom she had grimly 'suspected', sat together in debative conversation in one corner of the room. Every once in a while a phrase she could understand touched her ear. She heard 'slave trade' and 'violent overthrow' and 'off de pig', an expression she'd never heard before. One of the women, the only one of this group to acknowledge her, laughingly asked if she had come to 'join the revolution'. She had stood shaking by the door, trying so hard to understand she felt she was going to faint. Jerome rose from among the group of men, who sat in a circle on the other side of the room, and, without paying any attention to her, began reciting some of the nastiest-sounding poetry she'd ever heard. She left the room in shame and confusion, and no one bothered to ask why she'd stood so long staring at them, or whether she needed anyone to show her out. She trudged home heavily, with her head down, bewildered, astonished, and perplexed.

And now she hunted through her husband's clothes looking for a clue. Her hands were shaking as she emptied and shook, pawed and sometimes even lifted to her nose to smell. Each time she emptied a pocket, she felt there was something, *something*, some little thing that was escaping her.

Her heart pounding, she got down on her knees and looked under the bed. It was dusty and cobwebby, the way the inside of her head felt. The house was filthy, for she had neglected it totally since she began her search. Now it seemed that all the dust in the world had come to rest under her bed. She saw his shoes; she lifted them to her perspiring cheeks and kissed them. She ran her fingers inside them. Nothing.

Then, before she got up from her knees, she thought about the intense blackness underneath the headboard of the bed. She had not looked there. On her side of the bed on the floor beneath the pillow there was nothing. She hurried around to the other side. Kneeling, she struck something with her hand on the floor under his side of the bed. Quickly, down on her stomach, she raked it out. Then she raked and raked. She was panting and sweating, her ashen face slowly colouring with the belated rush of doomed comprehension. In a rush it came to her: 'It ain't no woman.' Just like that. It had never occurred to her there could be anything more serious. She stifled the cry that rose in her throat.

Coated with grit, with dust sticking to the pages, she held in her crude, indelicate hands, trembling now, a sizeable pile of paperback books. Books that had fallen from his hands behind the bed over the months of their marriage. She dusted them carefully one by one and looked with frowning concentration at their covers. Fists and guns appeared everywhere. 'Black' was the one word that appeared consistently on each cover. *Black Rage, Black Fire, Black Anger, Black Revenge, Black Vengeance, Black Hatred, Black Beauty, Black Revolution.* Then the word 'revolution' took over. *Revolution in the Streets, Revolution from the Rooftops, Revolution in the Hills, Revolution and Rebellion. Revolution and Black People in the United States, Revolution and Death.* She looked with wonder at the books that were her husband's preoccupation, enraged that the obvious was what she had never guessed before.

How many times had she encouraged his light reading? How many times been ignorantly amused? How many times had he laughed at her when she went out looking for 'his' women?

With a sob she realised she didn't even know what the word 'revolution' meant, unless it meant to go round and round, the way her head was going.

With quiet care she stacked the books neatly on his pillow. With the largest of her knives she ripped and stabbed them through. When the brazen and difficult words did not disappear with the books, she hastened with kerosene to set the marriage bed afire. Thirstily, in hopeless jubilation, she watched the room begin to burn. The bits of words transformed themselves into luscious figures of smoke, lazily arching toward the ceiling. 'Trash!' she cried over and over, reaching through the flames to strike out the words, now raised from the dead in glorious colours. 'I kill you! I kill you!' she screamed against the roaring fire, backing enraged and trembling into a darkened corner of the room, not near the open door. But the fire and the words rumbled against her together, overwhelming her with pain and enlightenment. And she hid her big wet face in her singed then sizzling arms and screamed and screamed.

Judith Barrington

Poems

I am a victim of
migraines
insomnia
the taxman
my landlord
and patriarchal institutions which say
I am a deviant.
I am a victim of
my family
who think I am a
middle class
high spirited
ex-career-wife
who has turned a little
eccentric
(but knows how people like us behave).
I am a victim of
the garage
which lies to me about my car

because I am a woman
and cannot understand
these things;
and of men in cinemas
and tube trains
who whisper obscenities
while I cringe with illogical victim-guilt;
and of my mother
who died horribly
before I had time
to wish her gone,
leaving me
guilty
to search her out in my lovers
and hate her
for being a victim too,
and hate her more
for being a victim
of me.

No one can be a victim of me;
the guilt
will throttle or paralyse me
soon.
If you find yourself
under my feet
please don't notice
that I'm treading on you.

last night when you fell asleep
in my arms
your muscles twitched
for a long time.
I wanted to unravel them
gently with my fingers
strand by strand
and lay them tidily
on your bones

for a rest.

Marjorie Jackson

Dadda

Dadda had rolled up his trousers and was paddling in the sea. Joe paddled too, but you couldn't see much of his legs: only the ankles. Dadda's legs were lovely and brown. Nut-brown — like the bears in the Minty Hemlock stories.

Joe's ankles were white, with big bones that stood out, shiny and sharp. The ends of his trousers had got all wet from the waves. Joe didn't like people seeing his legs. He wasn't a cissy, or anything like that. Mother said something was wrong with his skin. He wasn't *allowed* to get brown.

I wondered if Joe's legs were hairy like Dadda's. He was really quite strong, even though he was pale. He always piggy-backed me back to our digs when they came out of the pub. And he was very funny. He knew the most super jokes and he was always making me laugh. I liked Joe — though not as much as Dadda of course. Dadda was tall, and he ran very fast — much faster than Joe; and his arms and legs were strong man's arms and legs — sunburned and fuzzy, with wiry, dark hair. When I grew up, that's what I wanted more than anything else in the world: lovely long hair on my arms and my legs; crispy-brown hair — like Dadda had.

Mother always sat in a deck chair on the dry sand, knitting or reading a book. She stayed all the time while we paddled and played: just sat by herself.

Joe's wife couldn't come because she helped her sister who had a cafe on the promenade. She had to make tea and help to wash up. Joe slept there on a camp bed on a bathroom floor. I'd heard Mother say — and what a pity it was, Joe being such a kind helpful man! I don't think Dadda would *ever* have slept on a floor — but then, I don't suppose anyone would ever have asked him to.

Every afternoon I had the two men all to myself. It was nice to be with the men — much more interesting than sitting with Mother. Mother could never understand it. She thought it would be much more ladylike if I sat by her side and learned to do knitting and embroidery; but I didn't want to be a lady. Ladies had dull, boring lives. I wanted to be a boy — strong as a horse and brave as a man. I wanted to climb and jump and splash in the sea, and play cricket on the sands, and throw stones farther than the men. All the lovely exciting things that boys did. And Dadda liked me to do boys' things.

Dadda was doing cartwheels at the edge of the sea — making all the ladies laugh. The ladies always said how nice he was — but when they said it to mother she just looked mysterious and didn't say anything back.

He was very good at cartwheels, Dadda. Better than me — and much better than Joe. He did lots of cartwheels in a great circle, and all the money fell out of his pocket, and the ladies laughed and picked it up and took it back to him, and he gave them big smacking kisses and told them to keep it and buy themselves ice-cream: and everyone was so happy.

After the games we had to go back. Mother waved from her chair. Mother always knew when things had to be done. Dadda always forgot.

Joe picked up the ball and the bucket and spade, and Dadda swung me up on his back and galloped barefoot over the stones and down to the sea.

The ladies all screamed as he made great big waves, soaking

their clothes. But Dadda laughed and gave them a wink — and they didn't seem to mind after that. Some of the husbands looked cross though. I don't think husbands like Dadda much.

Then, dripping with sea, we galloped back up the sands to Mother's deckchair, and Dadda dropped me, upside down — plonk, at her feet. You could tell she was cross from the look on her face. Dadda had dropped me down wet each day that week, and still he forgot that it made her so cross.

The sand stuck all over my legs and wet hair, and it took Mother ages getting it off. Mother didn't say anything, though, because Joe was there; and Joe turned away and pretended to read the paper. My dress was all right because of the waders. I always had to wear waders over my dress. They were supposed to keep me dry. I was only allowed to swim once a day. It was always waders in the afternoon. They were made of blue rubber with elasticy legs, and looked like my baby cousin's rompers. No one else wore them, but Mother said *I* had to — so nothing could be done.

After she'd cleaned me, Joe packed up the bag. He folded the towels and waders and put them neatly inside, then put down the deck chair.

Dadda was amusing the children by standing on his hands. They all crowded round. He could stay upside down for ages and ages — quite still except for his wiggling toes. Little girls were puffing, trying to blow him down, and he pulled funny faces and made them laugh. The boys were all trying to copy — but no one could do it like him.

He was very athletic, Dadda was. He could swim right out past the end of the pier till you could hardly see where he was. But Mother worried. She used to call out for him to come back, but that just made him laugh and swim away fast, so she didn't say anything now. She just sat, reading her book and worrying quietly. Mother was always expecting a disaster.

Joe fastened my sandals and hoisted me up on his back, and Dadda left his shirt off and walked on his hands right to the end of the prom.

Joe had a motorbike and sidecar and every teatime he ran us

back to our digs. I had to sit in the sidecar with Mother, and Dadda sat behind Joe.

It was beautifully noisy and people all stopped and watched us start up. Old ladies put their fingers in their ears and grumbled and went rigid and said it shouldn't be allowed, we'd made everyone deaf, but Dadda would blow them a kiss and then it was all right.

After tea, Joe's wife had finished her work and everyone went to the pub. I went there too but I couldn't go in. I'd sit on the step with a bottle of pop. Mother fussed and came to see how I was, but Dadda was scornful and said I could take care of myself.

Men sometimes tickled my face and called me a pretty little lady, and mothers tutted and said poor little soul and wasn't-it-a-pity-some-people-didn't-have-more-sense-of-responsibility!

I always tried to look happy, though, in case they were sorry and brought me *their* girls to play with. I hated playing with girls. Girls were so dull. They did odd bits of knitting in horrible pink wool, and showed off their knickers and told lies, and cried when they fell down. You'd think a cut knee was the end of the world! Dadda wouldn't have liked it if I'd cried when I fell down. He was always saying brave men never cry. Only babies and cissies cried. So I never cried. Not about things like that anyway — not about cut knees. It was only inside hurts that made me cry — and then only in the dead of night when nobody else could possibly know.

One morning we met Joe at the end of the prom. He'd been having trouble with his bike. Dadda said *he'd* soon put it right and prodded and poked and looked very wise, but I don't think he *really* knew how motorbikes worked. Then he said if Joe didn't mind he'd give it a test. I'd never seen Dadda drive a motorbike before but I supposed that he must have been able to or he wouldn't have said.

It was quiet in the mornings there on the prom; right at the end where the toilet-block was. Just a drinking fountain for people and a trough for the dogs. There weren't any dogs though; just pigeons. Lots and lots of pigeons.

Dadda got on the bike and I watched the birds. A bag of squashed sandwiches fell off the bin and the birds strutted round and ate the bits. They had pink feet and they made friendly whirring noises between bites.

Dadda kicked the starter and they all flew away in a lumpy grey cloud banging their wings. They circled round twice then landed again on the toilet-block roof.

Dadda had to start the bike quite a few times before it went properly. Joe didn't look pleased.

Dadda laughed and turned his cap back to front and borrowed Mother's sunglasses, and hunched over the handle-bars and pretended to be a racing driver. He shot off very fast and went right round the block calling brrmm ... brrmm ... brmmm.

I saw the pigeon by the dustbin when Dadda rode round for the second time. It couldn't fly. It kept walking out to the middle of the road. I bit on my lip and clutched at my dress till some fingernails broke. It couldn't fly! I didn't want to look but I was scared to not-look and my head wouldn't think and my body wouldn't move. There was nothing at all I could do.

Dadda was laughing and whooping and standing up on the bike. He swerved right in and he just missed the bird. He did it on purpose — you could tell that.

I wanted to cry; and I knew I must not cry or I'd make Dadda cross. So I ran out in the road and called out shoo ... shoo. And the bird stood and looked and walked round in a ring.

Dadda came back on the terrible bike, his face all laughing and waving his arm. And he swerved right over to the wrong side of the road, and he took careful aim, and went wheeeeee like the men in the cowboy films; and the front wheel went bump — right over the bird.

I just stood there and screamed, and Mother rushed up thinking Dadda was killed; and I was sick all over the road.

When Mother saw that Dadda was all right she picked me up crossly and took me into the ladies and said couldn't I have waited until she'd got me inside. And I sat down on the little lavatory that was specially for children, and cried and cried for a long, long time.

When she knew what I was crying for, Mother said don't be so foolish — the pigeon would be up in heaven by now and much happier than walking about on the earth with a poor broken wing!

When we came out Dadda was still laughing and talking to Joe. And he looked at me sorrowfully and said Child! — who'd have believed it; an offspring of mine bawling because of a bird — a scavenging bird; just vermin, that's all! And I managed to get my mind into the won't-think-about-it now way like I'd done in hospital.

Joe cuddled me and piggy-backed me to the paper stall and bought me a comic; and I didn't go swimming with Dadda that day. I sat by Joe on the beach reading comics and watching Mother knit.

The next day we had to go home and it was quite a long time before I saw Joe again.

It was just after tea, and Dadda was cutting the grass for the lady with the lovely furry coat who lived over the back. You could see him from the kitchen window, walking up and down, down and up — pushing the mower. He'd rolled up the sleeves of his white shirt and his arms looked so lovely and brown. I wished my arms would get brown like his.

The motorbike made the telly picture go all wobbly and I knew as soon as it stopped that it was Joe. He'd brought a brown pup. It had wandered into their house but they couldn't keep it because Joe's wife was at work. It was such a pretty thing, and as it would be my birthday soon Joe had brought it for me.

Mother looked at Joe in a rather strange way — then they both looked at Dadda cutting grass. I hugged the dog and Mother looked rather sad; nobody spoke.

Then Dadda came and slapped Joe on the back. He lifted the dog by the scruff of the neck and sighed loudly and said Jesus Christ — not another bloody female!

At bedtime I settled her into a chair, and Dadda looked cross and said get it off there. We'll have no molly-coddling in this house! The shed's the place for a dog.

So I took her outside and found a box in the shed. The next day when Dadda went to work we brought it inside. And Mother laughed and called her Dog-wog because we couldn't think of a suitable name. I said wasn't she just like the bears in the Minty Hemlock stories she used to read me when I was small — all cuddly and warm with soft nut-brown fur; she laughed and said yes and gave Dog-wog some food. Still we couldn't think of a proper name.

When Mother went to the shops, Dog-wog peed on the rug. It made big, faded patches all over the mat. And in the afternoon she scratched the paint off the dining-room door.

When Dadda came home, he saw right away and was cross. Then Dog-wog snatched Dadda's slipper out of his hand, and Dadda shouted and shouted and hit the dog with the lead, and said we're not having this — it can clear off tonight. And Mother said you can't just put it out on the street, and Dadda said can't I, we'll see about that!

And just before bedtime he got down the tin bath that hung on the wall out in the yard and started filling it with water. I said what was he going to do? He said mind your own business and get off to bed. A terrible fear came over me, and I said you're not going to do anything to Dog-wog, are you? And he said just you shut up and get off to bed.

I stood in the yard and I screamed and screamed. He smacked me very hard and carried me into the kitchen and said it was about time I grew up and accepted a few facts of life!

I tried to be reasonable — the way he liked. I offered him my most treasured possession — the wrist-watch that Grandad gave me just before he died. And he said be your age child — did I really think he was going to have the home ruined because of a dog? Mother started to cry and Dadda said bloody women — they'd drive you to drink! And he snatched me up and shook me, and locked me in my bedroom.

All that night I just lay there on top of the bed. I didn't take my clothes off at all.

I heard Dadda filling the bath out in the yard. The squeak of the tap as a bucket was filled. The whoosh of the water as he tipped it into the bath with his big, strong, brown arms. Time after time. Then the scratch of the iron bucket on the flagstones as he kicked it away. Then a few small whimpers. Some splashes. Then nothing at all. I lay very still and thought — now Dog-wog's dead.

All through that awful night the thought went right round my body — again and again. I had to keep trying to hold it away. Not to let it get near the hurting part.

And sometimes, in the night, I could manage for quite a long time not thinking at all.

All this was a long time ago, when I was small. I was thinking about it today because last night I had a dream.

Last night I dreamed we were back at the sea. And I sat in a boat and watched Dadda swim past … left right … left right, with his strong hairy arms.

And just as he'd passed, his face screwed up, and he threw up his arms, and buckled with pain. He turned round to face me and called out for help; but I just turned away and looked back at the shore. When I looked round again, Dadda was still — his arms stretched out wide, his eyes fixed on the sky.

I sat there a long, long time — just watching him float. Down up … up down, with the lap of the tide.

He would have been proud of my cool, grown-up ways. I didn't feel sad and I didn't cry out.

You could tell he'd been strong even now he was still. Some seaweed had drifted and caught on his feet and got all tangled up in his brown arms and legs. Nut-brown — like the bears in the Minty Hemlock stories.

Natalia Baranskaya

Translated by Pauline Jaray

A Week Like Any Other

       At the end of 1969 the Soviet literary magazine
Novy Mir *published a story which portrayed in diary form one
week in the life of Olga, a young mother trying to hold down a
demanding job, bring up small children and keep her marriage
together. The story touched a sore spot for many Russians and
raised pressing questions about a society where eighty percent
of women work outside the home; about the way women were
expected to do all the housework, the primitive contraception
then available, the shortcomings of State nursery care. 'A Week
Like Any Other' raised storms of argument and flooded
newspapers with letters for months after its publication.*

  *The following excerpt begins at the plant where Olga works.
She has just been warned by her boss to be more punctual and
is anxious about her job. A questionnaire about working
mothers and absenteeism circulated round the factory has
increased her worries.*

Lucy Markoryan can see something's wrong. She puts her arm
round my shoulders and draws me to her. Rocking me back
and forth she says:

'Don't get upset, Olya, they won't give you the sack ... '

'They'd never dare to sack her, with two children,' Luska suddenly boils up. 'First they'd have to give her a reprimand, and so far there's only one black mark against her.'

That was for being late, too.

I'm beginning to feel ashamed. Luska is kind and sympathetic really — and I've been wanting to avoid talking about my affairs in front of her.

'Listen, girls, you have to understand how frightened I am all the time. I'm terrified I won't get my experiments finished. The deadline's in a month.'

'OK, but don't get so *neurotic* about it', Lucy Markoryan cuts in.

'What do you mean "don't get neurotic"?' Luska flings at her. 'You can see what she's going through. Why can't you help her calm down and stop worrying? But really, Olya, you shouldn't take it to heart like that. I mean it. You'll see, everything will work out all right.'

There's a catch in my throat. What sweet simple words. If I start howling now, that'll be it. Lucy rescues me.

'Listen, my lovelies,' she says, with a brisk pat on our shoulders, 'How about arranging a three-way exchange? Luska takes my flat, I move to Olga's, and Olga to Luska's place.'

'And then what?' we ask, puzzled.

'No, that's not it ... ' Lucy Markoryan draws diagrams in the air. 'No, this is how it should be: Olya moves to me, I go to Luska, and Luska to Olya. Then we'll all have what we need.'

Luska laughs. 'You want to swap your three-room flat for one room in a communal flat?'

'No, I don't want to ... but it would be more suitable. I lose out on living space and mod cons — there's no bathroom, is there? There is? But on the other hand I gain on more important things. You wouldn't lose out either, Luska — Olya's Dima is wonderful. My Suren will be happy with the arrangement — Olya's younger than me, and curvier. And I need a granny for babysitting, how I need one! Well — how about it?'

Luska flares up. 'Oh, get lost. You never take anything

seriously.' She turns to go, but simultaneously the door opens and Luska nearly collides with Marya Matveevna.

'Comrades, what a noise you're making,' says Marya Matveevna in her deep voice. 'You're disturbing our work. Has something happened?' I grab for Luska's hand, and not a moment too soon — she's just opening her mouth ready to pour out our entire conversation to M.M. (that's what we call Marya Matveevna among ourselves). We all respect Marya Matveevna. We admire her integrity. But talking to her about down-to-earth things is impossible. We know exactly what she's going to say beforehand. We see her as an old idealist: it seems to us that somehow she's abstracted herself, or something. She's simply not in touch with ordinary everyday life, but soars high above it, like a bird. Her life story is extraordinary: at the beginning of the thirties she worked in an industrial commune, in the forties she was at the front, and then in the political division. She lives alone — her daughters, brought up in a children's home, have long since had their own children. Marya Matveevna lives only for her work — her industrial work, her party work. She's seventy.

So we admire her for her merits — who could do otherwise?

'So what's going on here? she says severely.

'Well, actually we're picking Olya to pieces,' Lucy smiles.

'What about?'

'Her lateness,' Luska puts in quickly. A mistake.

Marya Matveevna shakes her head reproachfully. 'And I believed you.' I feel uneasy, and I can see the others do too. You can't behave this way with M.M.

'Look Marya Matveevna,' I say sincerely, though I don't actually answer her question, 'it's funny how things work. I have two children, and I feel confused about it ... I feel awkward about it somehow — twenty-six years old and two children, as if this were ...'

'A pre-revolutionary remnant,' Lucy prompts.

'What are you saying, Lucy!' Marya Matveevna says indignantly.

'Don't talk nonsense, Olya. You should be proud that you're

a good mother — and what's more, a good worker. You're a true Soviet woman!'

M.M. talks, and I ask myself why I should be proud. Am I such a good mother? Do I deserve praise as a worker? And what does 'true Soviet woman' really mean? It's no good asking Marya Matveevna any of this — she won't respond.

We set M.M.'s mind at rest by telling her I'm just in a bit of a depression, a mood which will pass.

We go back to our room. I didn't even get any clear information about the form — when has it got to be returned, and to whom? But now a note is handed to me: 'They will collect the questionnaire from us all next Monday. They want our opinion. They might have questions. And what about the questions we might have? Lucy M.' Right. That's enough about the questionnaire for now.

I look for Friday's results in the report sheets and copy the last experiments out on a sheet of paper — for Lucy Markoryan. Then I take another sheet as large as a newspaper and rule lines on it. This will be a summary table of all the experiments that have been made. It's compiled according to the data in our report sheets. The first composition of our glass-fibre-reinforced plastics showed increased brittleness. We finished working on the formulation of the binder resins. Then we started the second series of tests. And then everything from the beginning again: hygroscopicity, water resistance, heat resistance, thermostability, fire resistance ... I never imagined such carefulness, accuracy and attention could be devoted to sewage pipes and roofs.

Once, long ago, I had a talk with Lucy about this. I admitted I was dreaming about getting into a different laboratory. Lucy laughed. 'Today's youth are funny, they all want to go in for space engineering — but who's going to put life on earth in order?' And suddenly she asked, 'Have you never lived in a house where the sewage leaks out of rusty old pipes onto people's heads, and where the ceilings are coming down?' It turned out that both of us had. Only I hadn't given it much thought.

161

The more time I spend with the new reinforced plastics the more interested I get. Now I can't wait to finish the testing of the new composition. How will it stand up to the stresses? How strong will it be? But right now there's this congestion in the mechanics lab. Congestion and bottleneck.

But everything else is going normally. Here I am starting to fill in the table with data from the physico-chemical tests — they're nearly completed. Slowly I fill in the columns of figures, leaf through the report sheets. Water resistance. Specimen No. 1 ... Specimen No. 2 ... Specimen No. 3 ... all in milligrammes ... time of immersion, 15 hrs 20 mins, drying time 15 hrs 20 mins, weight after conditioning ... The fingers of my left hand are holding the ruler on the relevant page, my right hand copies down the figures — the average of the results of the three tests — on to the table.

I have to work concentratedly, making no mistakes.

'Olya, Olya.' A quiet voice interrupts me. 'It's ten to two, I'm going out. Tell me what you want.'

Today it's Shura's turn to do the shopping for the 'mums'. Our arrangement is that every day one of us does the shopping for the rest. And we asked to have our lunch break from two till three, when there are fewer people in the shops. I order butter, milk, a kilo of flour, and a bun to eat here. I won't go out, I'll work — I've lost too much time already today.

Lucy has disappeared. I think she's trying to make up for lost time too.

I was right. She appears ten minutes before the end of the break. Her dress and her hair smell of varnish — the familiar smell of our GRP. She's as hungry as a wolf, so we share my sausage and the bun, washing them down with water from the lab tap.

I get absorbed in my table again. The second half of the day passes so quickly and imperceptibly that at first I don't realise why our 'quiet' room has suddenly got so noisy. It turns out that everybody is getting ready to leave.

Now, on to the bus — jammed again — and then the

underground, and the frantic change of trains. Once again I've got to rush like mad, I can't be late: my family gets home before seven.

On the underground I travel in style — standing in the corner by a closed door. I stand and yawn. I yawn so much that the guy next to me can't resist a remark.

'What were you up to last night, love?'

'I rocked my kids to sleep,' I retort, to get rid of him.

I yawn and remember this morning. Monday morning. At a quarter to six the telephone rang, it rang for a long time. Nobody went to answer it. I didn't want to get up either. No, it wasn't the phone, it was the doorbell. A telegram? From Auntie Vera, maybe? Perhaps she is coming to visit? I flew into the entrance hall. The telegram lay on the floor, open, but there wasn't a word on it, just small holes, like on a punchcard. I floated effortlessly above the blank telegram, and turned to go back to bed. Only then did it sink in that the ringing was the alarm clock, so I told it briskly to get stuffed. It stopped at once. It was getting very quiet. Dark, so dark and so quiet ...

But I jumped up, dressed quickly, all the hooks on my girdle immediately found their loops, and — miraculously — even the torn-off hook had been sewn on. I ran into the kitchen to put the kettle on and the water for this evening's macaroni. Another miracle — the gas rings flared, the water in the pan bubbled, the kettle sang. It whistled like a bird, fuit-fu, fuit-fu ... and then I understood: it wasn't the kettle whistling but my nose. But I couldn't wake up. Then Dima started shaking me. I felt his hand on my back rocking me, and he said:

'Olya, love, oh Olya, *please* wake up this time, or you'll have to run like mad again.'

And then I really did get up: I dressed slowly, the hooks of my girdle couldn't find the eyes, and one of them was torn off. I went into the kitchen, tripped on the rubber mat in the entrance hall and very nearly fell. There was no gas, and the match went out, burning my fingers. I'd forgotten to turn the main valve on. At last I made it to the bathroom. After my wash I buried my face in the warm Turkish towel. For half a

163

second it was like falling asleep again, and I woke up with the words: 'Damn the lot of it!'

But that's just rubbish. What is there to damn and blast at? Everything's great. We've got a flat in a new house, Kotka and Gulka are gorgeous, Dima and I love each other, and I have an interesting job. There's *nothing* in my life I'd want to get rid of. Not a thing. Never!

Tuesday

Today I get up normally — at ten past six I'm ready, except for my hair. I peel potatoes for supper, stir the porridge, make coffee, warm the milk, wake Dima, and go to get the children up. I switch the light on in the nursery and call: 'Good morning, sweetiepies!' — but they snooze on. I pat Kotka, cuddle Gulka, then I strip their blankets off. 'Time to get up!' Kotka gets on his knees and buries his nose in the pillow. I take Gulka in my arms, she kicks me off with her feet, and howls. I call for Dima to help me, but he's shaving. I leave Kotka alone; Gulka has stopped kicking. I pull on her vest, her knickers, her dress, but she slips off my knees on to the floor. Something's hissing in the kitchen — blast, I forgot to turn the milk off. I sit Gulka on the floor and race for the kitchen.

'What a state you get yourself in,' says a freshly-shaved, handsome Dima, emerging from the bathroom.

I haven't got time to reply. Gulka, abandoned, starts up with new strength. Her howls wake Kotka at last. I give Gulka her bootees, she calms down and, groaning and puffing, starts to twist and turn them round her fat little legs. Kotka dresses himself, but so slowly that it's impossible to wait. I help him, doing my hair at the same time: Dima is laying the table for breakfast. He can't find the sausage in the fridge, and calls for me. While I run to Dima, Gulka pinches my comb and hides it. I haven't time to look for it, so I pin up my half-combed hair, get the children washed somehow, and we sit down to eat. The children have milk and a bun; Dima eats a proper breakfast, but I can't, I just gulp down a coffee.

It's ten to seven already, and Dima is still eating. It's time to

164

get the children into their outdoor clothes, quickly, both at once, so that they won't start sweating.

'Let me finish my coffee,' Dima grumbles.

I sit the children on the settee, drag the whole heap of clothes in and start working on both at once: a pair of socks, another pair of socks, one pair of trousers, another pair, sweater and cardigan, one scarf, and another, mittens, and ...

'Dima, where are Kotka's mittens?'

'How do I know?' he answers, but rushes off to look for them; he finds them in the most unlikely place — the bathroom. That's where he threw them last night. I squeeze two pairs of feet into boots, pull caps on to wriggling little heads; racing against time, I shout at them as if they were horses I was trying to harness: 'Stand still, whoa, stand, will you!' Here Dima lends a hand, he puts on their winter coats, ties their mufflers round them and fastens their belts. I get dressed, can't get my foot into one boot — ah, so this is where my comb was!

At last we get out. Our last words to each other: 'Have you locked the door?' 'Have you got money?' 'Don't run like a lunatic.' 'OK, don't be late fetching the children.' And we part.

It's five past seven, and, needless to say, I'm on the run. From our hill I can see in the distance how long the bus queue's growing. I tear down the hill and flap my arms to keep my balance on the slippery path. The bus always arrives crammed full, and takes in about five people from the queue, and then a few daredevils rush it; usually someone's lucky and manages to grab the handrail; the bus pants, revs, and accelerates away with someone's leg, coat hem or briefcase still sticking out of the door.

Today I'm in with the tearaways. I have a flasback to my student years when I was the sprinter, the jumper, 'Olya the dynamo.' Gathering momentum on the ice I jump and grab, hoping that somebody else, somebody strong, does the same behind me and pushes me inside. And that's what happens. When I've got my breath back I manage to pull my *Youth* magazine out of my bag. I read Aksyonov's story — which everyone else read ages ago — about the oversupply of barrels. I don't understand everything in the story, but it's a laugh and it cheers me up. I even read on the escalator, and finish the last page at the bus stop. I manage to arrive at the research station on time.

First thing, of course, is to get hold of Valya in the mechanics lab. She gets annoyed:

'Why do you keep turning up here? I've told you before — nearer the end of the week.'

'Tomorrow, then?'

'No, the day after.'

She's right. Of course I shouldn't keep bothering her. But the others do as well, and if a gap did come up, it would be awful to miss it.

I go upstairs to our room and ask Luska to prepare specimens for tomorrow's tests in the electro lab. Then I sit down again to do my summary table. At half past twelve I go to the library to change journals and catalogues.

I always systematically look through American and English publications on building materials: I do it regularly in the library at the plant and — whenever I can spare the time to get there — at the Lenin Library, in the scientific, technical and patent departments. I'm glad that I've kept up my English ever since school. Leafing through magazines for twenty minutes or so after two or three hours work is a real relaxation, a real pleasure. I show everything that bears on our work to Lucy Markoryan and Jacob Petrovich. He knows English too, but not as well as I do. Today in the library I manage to scan through *Building Materials '68*, study the new issues of the *Abstracts*, and leaf through the catalogue of one American firm.

I look at my watch: five to two. I forgot my shopping order!

I run to our room, remembering on the way that I never finished combing my hair, and suddenly I get the giggles. Breathless and dishevelled I burst into our room, and find myself in the middle of a crowd — the room is full of people. A meeting? Could I have forgotten?

'Ah, very appropriate. Ask Olya Voronkova what influenced

her decision,' says Alla Sergeevna to Zinaida Gustavovna.

I can see from their faces that a heated argument is going on. About me? Have I done something wrong?

'A discussion about the questionnaire has developed,' Marya Matveevna explains. 'Zinaida raised an interesting question: will a woman — a Soviet woman, that is — be influenced by public interests when it comes to something like child-bearing?'

'And you want my expert opinion to help you decide?' I answer, relieved. (I thought it was something about my work.)

Of course I'm taken as the chief authority on childbirth, but I'm sick of it. Besides, Zinaida's 'interesting question' is simply a stupid question, even if you believe that she put it seriously. But knowing Zinaida and her bitchiness, it's much more likely that her question was just spiteful, that she wants to have a dig at somebody. Zinaida herself is at that fortunate age when you don't have children any more.

Shura explains in a whisper that the argument was about the fifth question on the form: 'If you have no children, state the reason: medical grounds, material domestic conditions, family circumstances, personal considerations, etc. (underline as applicable).' I don't understand why we're arguing when everyone can get round the question by underlining 'personal considerations'. I'd even underline 'etc.' But they all seem interested in the fifth question, and the childless ones in the room are even a bit threatened by it.

Alla Sergeevna calls it 'monstrous tactlessness'. Shura objects: 'No more than the whole questionnaire.'

Luska rushes to the defence: 'But surely it's necessary — to find a way out of a serious, even a dangerous, situation — a population crisis?'

Lydia, who's my rival for the junior scientist job and who has two admirers, says: 'Leave the crisis to the married ones. Let them deal with it.' Barbara Petrovna, calm and kind, corrects Lydia: 'If the problem is of general, public, importance then it concerns everyone ... below a certain age.'

Lucy shrugs her shoulders: 'Is it really worth arguing about something as hopeless as this questionnaire?'

Several voices ask at once: 'Why hopeless?'

Lucy argues that the compilers suggest basically personal motives as reasons for not having any children. This means that every family is ruled by personal considerations when they have a child, therefore 'no demographic investigations will succeed in influencing this process'.

'Look, you're forgetting "material domestic conditions",' I object. Marya Matveevna didn't like Lucy's sceptical remark. 'A great deal is being done in our country to free woman from her slavery, and there's no reason to mistrust the desire to do even more.'

'Maybe a strictly practical approach would bring the best results,' says Lucy. 'Now in France, the state pays the mother for each child. That's probably more effective than any amount of forms.'

'Pays? Like a pig farm?' Alla Sergeevna screws up her mouth in disgust.

'Watch your language!' M.M.'s manly voice rings out at exactly the same time as Luska's squeak: 'Are people the same as pigs to you, then?'

'But that's France, where they have capitalism,' Lydia shrugs.

All this fuss bores me. It's late. I'm starving. One of the mums has to go shopping. I still have to do my hair. And I've really had all I can take of that form. I hold up my hand for attention and strike a pose.

'Comrades. Please give a mother the floor! The mother of a large family! I promise you I had my two kids solely in the national interest. I challenge you all to a contest, and hope you'll beat me on quantity as well as quality of production! But now — for pity's sake — won't somebody get me something to eat...' I'd intended to raise a laugh, and finish off the argument that way. But some of them take offence and a squabble breaks out. Venomous remarks fly from all sides, voices are raised, drowning each other.

I can only catch snatches of phrases: ... 'turn an important thing into a circus', '...if the animal instinct prevails over reason ...', '... all childless people are selfish', '... they themselves spoil their lives', '... and who'll pay you your pensions if there aren't enough of the young generation to be workers', '... the only true woman is one who can have children', and even '... he who puts his head into a noose had better keep his mouth shut'(!)

And in all this chaos, two voices of reason. Marya Matveevna's angry one: 'This isn't a discussion, it's some kind of beargarden.' And Barbara Petrovna's calm one: 'Comrades, what on earth are you getting so heated about? After all, we've all had the freedom to choose.' Things quieten down a bit, and then Zinaida, petty woman, screeches: 'It's all very well for them, but when we have to be on duty for them, or drag ourselves round the factories when we're sent on an assignment, or spend the whole evening at a meeting, then it affects us as well.'

So ends our women's caucus on the questionnaire and childbearing. And suddenly I am sorry: we could have had a serious discussion, it could even have been interesting.

On the way home the conversation keeps coming back to me. 'Each of us chose for herself ...' Do we really choose so freely? I look back at when I was pregnant with Gulka.

Of course we didn't want another child. Kotka was still a baby. He wasn't eighteen months when I realised I was pregnant again. I was horrified. I cried. I registered for an abortion. But I didn't feel ill, like I did with Kotka — I felt better, I felt completely different. I told this to an elderly woman who was waiting with me in the doctor's waiting room. And suddenly she said: 'That isn't because it's the second one, it's because it's a girl this time.' I went home immediately. When I got home I told Dima: 'I'm going to have a little girl, I don't want an abortion.' He was indignant: 'Why do you listen to old wives tales!' He began to try and persuade me not to play the fool, but to go and get the necessary forms.

But I believed it, and I began to imagine a little girl, a fair-haired, blue-eyed one, just like Dima (Kotka has chestnut hair and brown eyes, like me). I saw the little girl running about in a short skirt, shaking her funny little plaits, nursing a doll. Dima got annoyed when I told him my fantasy and we quarrelled. Then came the last possible time for an abortion. We had a decisive talk. I said: 'I can't kill my little daughter just because she'll make our life harder,' and burst into tears. 'Don't howl, idiot. Well, all right then — have it, if you're so crazy for it. But you'll see — it'll be another boy.' And then Dima stopped, looked at me quietly for a long time and, hitting the table with his hand, made a resolution: 'Right then, it's decided — we'll have it; enough crying and quarrelling.' He hugged me. 'Oh well, Olya, if it's another boy, so what? That won't be so bad either ... it'll be company for Kotka.' But it was Gulka who was born, and from the start she was so pretty — so fair, and ridiculously like Dima.

I had to leave the factory where I'd only worked for six months. (I'd been sitting at home for a year already with Kotka, I nearly lost my diploma.) Dima took a second job teaching evening classes at a technical school. Again we had to count the pennies, eat only cheap food. I nagged Dima if he bought himself a packet of expensive cigarettes. Dima complained about not getting enough sleep. We sent Kotka to the creche (I couldn't cope with two on my own) but he was always ill and mostly at home.

Did I choose the right thing? No, of course not. Do I regret it? Not for a minute. I love them so much, the little terrors. And I rush to be with them. I run, the shopping bag flails about and bangs me on the knees. I get on to the bus, and my watch says seven o'clock already. They'll be home by now. If only Dima doesn't let them stuff themselves with bread and remembers to put the potatoes on.

I dash along the path, cross the wasteland, career up the stairs. Yes, he has — the children are chewing lumps of bread, Dima is oblivious, deep in a technical journal. I light all the gas rings: put the potatoes on, the kettle, the milk, throw the chops into the frying pan. Twenty minutes later supper's on the table.

We eat a lot. For me it's actually the first proper meal of the day. Dima doesn't get all that much at the canteen either. As for the children — who knows what they've eaten.

After their big meal the babes are quite worn out, they prop up their cheeks with their fists, their eyes clouded with sleepiness. We have to drag them straight into the bath and then put them to bed. By nine o'clock they're fast asleep.

Dima comes back to the table. He likes to drink his tea in peace, to look through the newspaper, and read. And I wash the dishes, then I wash the children's clothes — the trousers Gulka wears to the creche, dirty aprons, hankies. I mend Kotka's tights, he always wears them through at the knees. I get all the clothes ready for the morning, collect Gulka's things into a bag. Then Dima presents me with his overcoat — he's torn off another button in the underground. Then the floor has to be swept. And the rubbish taken out — that's Dima's job.

At last it's all done, and I go to take a shower. I always do, even if I'm sick with tiredness. After eleven I go to bed. Dima has already made up our divan. He goes off to the bathroom. With my eyes already closed I realise that I've forgotten to sew the hook on my girdle again. But no power on earth can drag me out from under that blanket.

Two minutes later I'm asleep. I can just hear Dima lying down, but I'm beyond opening my eyes or answering his questions, and I can't kiss him back when he kisses me. He winds the alarm clock. I shut out the noise of the ticking. In six hours this hellish gadget will explode.

Natasha Morgan

The nets

Tonight you have hung my room with nets.
They were there when I returned.
Nets, I saw, and laughed because I knew
you were nearby, and coming soon.

I am a liberated woman, and you
          hang nets in my room
Am I a mermaid, or a bird to be held?
In the dark of the early morning they fall,
the gentlest of capturings,
          like a veil.

The dawn is a red theatre for birds.
We sit in a red bus, travelling west.
You missed your train. There will be other trains.
I am leaning on your shoulder
          and dream.

He said: Mostly I feel like a tractor

I am a tractor
useful and physically strong,
but do not tax me.
I will not sing for you
or do a dance
except in the way tractors do.

I will keep famine from your hearth
and hum, turning the earth.
Incidentally, I feed birds with worms.
All kindness from me
is incidental.

You see these hands —
My mother came from Ireland.
They know what's what there, eh?
What's that you say?
I have no time for growing things.
I clear the area — see —
then hammer the seed home.

173

Rosemary Yates

Mouselike

Where is that gentle face? Something has died or gone into hiding, something timid scurried away into its little hole in the wall. I thought I saw a mouse earlier but then it was all a joke. The pillow-case is grubby, it's never been so grey and we've none clean. It didn't look so bad when I first got into bed. My hair will get dirty I know. I wish I had a nice clean, soft feathery one. Fit for an odalisque he beams. He says I look pretty, the mouth parts. I show a smile, but there's no smile inside. Yet it was there before. Whatever was there has died. I close my eyes, I lie back on a slab of frayed stretched sheets. The bare light is directly above but lying on my back it should be quicker. He leaves a sliding, wet trail on my face. I'm cold, I don't want to go on top of the bedclothes, nor take off my nightgown. Always an excuse he says with a sigh. But honestly, this time I am cold, I am tired. But what's the use — all he'll do is fret over my health and turn up the fire until I can't breathe. He comes down on top of me. I feel my hair sweep all over the pillow, sweeping all the dirt underneath. He crushes me with his weight. My breathing gets jerky and gives the wrong impression. He begins to work hard on me all over, as if he's forgotten I'm here. They all do, and now he does — where's that kind look of his, the gentle line of the mouth? I can't understand how it vanished, it must have scurried away too. I take his face in my hands and trace his mouth, I draw it back but I can't find it. Is it the harsh light that alters his face? Or can't I see for the smell of his spilt nicotine? I let his head go and he looks up surprised. I put my arms around him, hoping to be encouraging but I always forget to move them. He works hard on the body playing with it with his hands. When the light's off I'm a beautiful curved instrument, he hears the music even if I don't. But not for long: the black grotesque shapes loom over me and come down without warning. I can't see where he is next, I have to put the light on. A spring thrusts upwards into my back, I wriggle to miss its aim. I could do with some water. Stop a minute. I lean up on one arm and drink from a glass on the table. I drink while he goes rummaging around between my legs. My strap falls off my shoulder and for a second I'm quite randy lying there. A tickle and the little mouse squeaks, pattering around its hole. But he wrecks it when he comes up from down below like a drunken frogman. He asks and I have to take off my nightgown. Now I'm fully exposed. I'm so cold — no, I am cold honestly. Stripped of an excuse he says. What do you mean excuse? I daren't stop him too long I know what will happen if he thinks I'm not going along with him. We could be lying awake until three. I'm pulled down again and underneath. He tries to keep me warm with the sheets and his body but it won't work. I'm suffocating. He gets up on top of the body and is everywhere at once. The body's swamped with him, his awkward shyness is just awkwardness. He's all over the place, I tense slightly. His head comes down on mine and his collarbone rubs against my chin. He's so engrossed playing with the body's limbs. Where has he gone? This is what they all come down to. Against the silence he makes little groans. I wish the radio was on. I could listen to something. I reach over to the switch. He looks up suddenly — where has he been all the time? He looks so naively shocked, it's laughable. I want to put on something — anything — no I'm not fed up. Why should I be fed up? Hurriedly I put a kiss on his cheek, anxious he doesn't sag and drop limp. His neck is like any other. Like mine, like anyone's, white and smooth with the usual smell of soap. It works wonders and he's back noisier than ever, perhaps because we haven't done it for a while. He rubs the sides while the spring pushes up again. And the blaring light pulls apart my shut lids. His snorts and groans are exaggerated, he must have got them from a film. I listen to them when I should be steadying him, guiding him. I find it hard to do everything at once. I can't remember what to do. Now he starts rubbing up the body making for the big grab. I hate this all over groping they all do it, working up like this. If only they would stick to the sides. I tense when they start this, I clench when they near. I've always hated it. I dart back inside, there's no haven anywhere. I look down at these breasts drooping over the edge — what can they find there? Two lumps of flesh like anybody's, I can't see what the fuss is. But they can see something and come hunting for it, working up insatiably prodding and groping. They claw at my breasts. With my elbow I cleverly guide him aside, I congratulate myself. Midnight. Surely he's almost finished, he's holding out a long time. I feel so tired, it should be over soon if I can keep him at it. We must paint that ceiling it's so stained with his smoke! The light shows up all the smears. What's the matter, he says, looking at me as if something was very wrong. Nothing, nothing at all. Each time he looks down it all adds to the time I have to lie here. I try and keep him at it, I tighten my grip round his back. I must encourage him now we've come so far. But he always looks so lost when he looks at me as if I'd slipped under the bed and left him. I shan't be able to go much longer if he keeps stopping, my tactics are failing, but he becomes more vigorous. His knees run up and down my legs like knobs of marble, it makes me weary. He pokes his way inside and I sigh with relief. I watch his backside move up and down under the sheets. He pushes hard trying to split me open but the whole thing's no thrill just ridiculous. It ought to be over by

176

now, I move my hands across his back mechanically while he tunnels in and out, up and down, making me more and more drowsy. Every now and then he stops and sighs, he deceives me, I think it's all over. Then all at once he's at the body's breasts again, his mouth sticking like a limpet. I wake up and clench, I use my elbow to drive him away but he's not having any. He just doesn't see, he doesn't care — don't! That's all I said, I didn't want you to stop. He halts abruptly and flops onto the bed and doesn't speak. He lies there ages, now and then he makes these stunted movements. I'm not sorry, or bothered.

Don't be so melodramatic! But saying that has no effect, we'll be awake hours. I lie fairly comfortable now we've come to the end of it and follow a faint line on the wall opposite. Lost in its hole the little mouse sleeps. I'm whitewashed with fatigue, I plead: I didn't mean you to stop, idiot, I was cold. Emptied I put my stare anywhere. He closes his eyes, placing his arm over them. Then he looks at me with all these faces saying all these things, I half hear their echoes later. The trouble is you've had a stupid upbringing, you're frigid, you really are. I say nothing, you really are goes on and on. Almost two-thirty and the light still on, and having to get up so early. I look over at him, quietly he's taken his hands away. In his profile I catch traces of his other half. I can feel mischief curdle inside at what would be so unexpected. Quickly without a second thought, I tickle his cheek with my tongue, but nothing. The mischief comes up bubbling, the only thing alive in the room. I kiss him, but nothing, not a flicker. His impassivity is encouraging, I feel quite awake, expectant, it's up to me. I tease him but he won't open his eyes. I take his head in my arms, it's both heavy and immovable but strangely fragile. I begin to recognise it, I recognise the fall of the eyebrows and begin to kiss them. I climb on top of him as slowly, as seductively as I can but it's hard when the sheets are so tight, and he's playing this hard-to-get stunt. I astonish us both by flinging the bedclothes back disdainfully. Fully exposed to the bare room he still lies unmoved. I'm in where it's too deep — now what am I to do? This mischief fades so quickly. I'm left exasperated — he won't do anything. Am I to do everything? I sink my head on his shoulder and plead with my cheek. But no, he doesn't stir, he's an impassable mountain, even below me he's weighing me down. He's not teasing or sulking, he seems to be waiting. With a dread I move my mouth over his face and neck; I expect to be flung aside. I don't know whether to leave little kisses or one long lick. I begin nibbling his chest but it's only a mouth on a chest — anyone's anywhere, no matter how hard I try. I don't mind him like this but I half wait for some kind of explosion, he isn't still inside. Am I trespassing? I try everything to rouse him, almost defeated I stroke him and he stirs. He comes awake in my arms, his vulnerable slenderness fills my arms, he's a wounded bird. My hands follow his shape, I'm there centred in each of them moving over his slim shape. His nakedness against mine excites me, a burning liquid begins to run. I seem to be flowering. My breasts hold full and firm on his chest. I curve round him, I fondle, caress, recognise him. I discover his hair. I close my eyes and know him in the dark. He is so real, so near, I can hardly tell where we cease to join. The fire running inside me seeks out an opening. He puts his arms around me and holds me, gingerly I excite him. But he becomes more and more lively, he anticipates me, he wants to be the first. The more vigorous he is the more I harden. From below he overwhelms, involuntarily I back out slowly. He rises over me in unquestionable movements, he's above me, it's irreversible. I lie down on my side again, under the bare light. His hand goes about handling. My face is fixed, I'm rooted, he's taking over. I push him back and climb on top, I want to see that face again. He's too earnest he prods and leaves me out. He's changed it's all gone. I have to think hard what to do, how to bring it all back. I go over my movements I study his face, I move the mouth, the brows, but it's gone. He eats me away, rubs me away. I scurry away into my hole, I leave nothing outside. What's the matter — nothing. I take hold of his head to show there's nothing wrong. But I leave it, I let it fall on the pillow. You're fed up. No I'm not. I don't feel anything, he doesn't believe me anyway. He sinks down on to the bed hopelessly falling limp. He seems exhausted, deadened. There's no movement, he lies there motionless. I climb up again. I take him, I lie on him almost crushing. He can hardly breathe. He's so lethargic it's easy to tickle him without caring about anything happening. With a thrill I see him lie there like helpless prey, a conquest. I tantalise and he doesn't respond. I wander down his face drawing in different lines about the mouth; this is my lover, this beautiful slender body. I stretch up to see him better. But he looks away at the ceiling his eyes half-closed. All I see is myself cringing above a vacant dummy, I fall back on the bed stranded. He looks over at me without sympathy.

Dolly Barrett

The Same Day in Westport and Knightsbridge

They had known each other in boarding school in
Gloucestershire. Sally was there against her will. Her father
had sent her from Westport, Connecticut when she was sixteen,
in the hope that she would go on to Cambridge. So she (freckle-
faced, big-breasted, having screwed three college boys and a
black baseball player) was sent to a girls' school full of hostile,
chaste Anglo-Saxons who were all well versed in the original
Ovid, all heirs to their mothers' pudding thighs. There were
catty arguments where some pallid, spiteful Classicist with no
real knees and a square ass would say, 'And I bet you
masturbate too!'

'Sure I masturbate,' Sally would reply and for weeks she was
the object of giggling and speculation.

But when she got to know Jessie, things became bearable,
even enjoyable. Jessie was tall and very thin with cropped hair.
Her father was dead and her mother was an embarrassment to
her; she was fifty-two years old, smoked until her grey forelock
turned brown, was obese, smelled of cabbage, tasted of salt.
Her teeth were large and yellow, the capillaries on her cheeks

were broken. She would sit after dinner and pick the strings of meat out of her back teeth with a fingernail. Jessie hated the idea of having turned in the liquids of that body. On her mother's face she saw her every bad feature exaggerated. The nose (that same chunky crookedness) was there on a huge scale.

Jessie liked school because it gave her an escape from her mother and now it had given her Sally with whom she could break the rules and talk for hours after lights out.

In November Sally started reading Betty Friedan and stopped talking about the black baseball player. They would take *The Feminine Mystique* and a pack of Gauloises outside at night. They sat in the bushes by the back road and Sally read aloud by the light of the street lamp. They inhaled smoke deeply and listened to the muffled voices of the matrons searching for them in the dormitory.

In April, as they were walking to class, Sally leapt on a bus and yelled 'Come on! It's going to Winchomb and I've three pounds in my pocket.' Jessie ran and jumped on the bus as it pulled out.

They came back four days later when the three pounds had run out and it had started to rain. It was Monday morning and Sally (who was older and considered to be the leader of the two) was called to the headmistress's office. She stood before the desk with her feet together and her hands behind her back. She looked unusually tidy.

'And where did you sleep, Sally?' asked the headmistress, a big-boned ungainly woman with an air of decay about her.

'In a field. In a sleeping-bag.'

'Where did you get the sleeping bag?'

'I ripped it off from a sporting goods store.'

'And did you both sleep in the sleeping-bag?' the headmistress asked, chanting over and over in her head 'I am a woman. She is a child. I am a woman. She is …'

'Yes.'

'Did you sleep in your school uniforms?'

'No. We slept in the raw.'

The headmistress flinched and tilted her head to one side.

She felt especially ungainly that day. Some days she felt whole and strong and tidy. As if everything fitted. Other days, like today, she felt porous, endless, without confines or definition. On those days she was filled with embarrassment and self-hatred ('... a child. I am a woman. She is a child. I am ...') Endeavouring to collect herself, the headmistress talked severely to Sally about the teachings of Jesus Christ and about Law and Order. But under her lecture and her unmentionable suspicions, she was utterly in awe of Sally who stood still, admitted everything and had exquisite legs.

Jessie never saw Sally after that. She sometimes wrote letters but never mailed them, even when she was twenty-six. It had been eleven years and no one had loved or understood her like Sally. She didn't mail them because Sally would probably be married by now. She probably laughed about those things at cocktail parties. They probably would no longer have any affinity.

Jessie spent another two years in boarding school and then went to the University of London. In the summer between school and university she went home to look after her dying mother.

On the last day she was looking through the bedroom drawers for angina pills. Her mother lay gasping on the bed. The room was filled with her smell. Jessie opened a drawer full of old lipsticks and discarded, unwashed nylon stockings. At the bottom of the drawer were three sheets of paper. She recognised them. They were pages of her poetry that she (a passionate, sebacious, disappointed fourteen-year-old) had thrown into the dustbin. Her poems. Her bad poems. That her mother, whose smell now filled the room, had retrieved tenderly, wiping off the tea-leaves, and kept for years. Which now, after years, were still bad, still smelled of garbage.

The pills were in the back of the drawer. She took one out of the bottle. Her mother's face had turned purple. She slipped it under the fat, wet tongue. She wiped her fingers on the back of her jeans. She couldn't help it.

The following week she took out a lease on a two-roomed flat in Knightsbridge. She had stayed in London ever since. After her degree she took a job in a large bookshop near the university. At twenty-six she was still in the flat, sharing the bed and the rent with a philosophy student named Arnold.

Sally was parcelled off to Westport shortly after her interview with the headmistress. She finished high school locally, went to college, dropped out as a junior and at twenty-seven was teaching ceramics and taking night classes to complete her degree. She had unhappy affairs with men from minority groups, all of whom were idealists and taller than she was. They never lasted long. They all left her with yellow love bites, purple scratches, someone else's smell in her blue jeans and the feeling that she must be far uglier on the inside than she was on the outside.

Jessie was awake at seven-thirty that morning in Knightsbridge. She sat on the windowsill with one thin leg sloping up to meet the wall.

She had dreamt but all she could remember was that it was unpleasant. 'It'll hang over me all day,' she said to herself and the sun slid from behind a cloud, turning the floorboards from grey to yellow.

She often dreamt of metamorphoses, people transforming as she ate lunch with them. She herself had once turned into an old man in a green tweed suit who gazed apologetically from the bathroom mirror. Sometimes people divided, became twins with identical hairstyles. Other times the original person had a duplicate, perhaps more fastidious than himself, who arrived late, having taken the time to straighten a bookshelf, trim a beard or tear the brown heads off a flowering plant.

But that morning she remembered nothing. As she awoke, her foot was falling heavily onto the iced surface of a puddle. Little white lines spreading in quick, geometrical progressions. She drew on a cigarette, the first thing since toothpaste, and felt a little dizzy. Her dream was gone. Smoke jetted out of her mouth in a blue-grey stream, then curled into a cloud. 'I am like the North Wind,' she thought.

On the mattress Arnold lay sleeping, the top sheet tangled round his left leg. Black hairs showed clearly on his long, pale body: on his arms and legs, running from his chest down his abdomen in odd patterns, like iron filings, then curling at his crotch. His thighs looked silly while he was sleeping. His genitals lay soft and defenseless and peculiar, she thought, like lychee fruit.

It seemed he had been lying there, morning after morning, with silly thighs, for a long time. It was over a year ago he used to come into the bookshop where she worked, never saying much, never pushing himself, but standing there eating yoghurt and looking at her achingly.

She often wondered why he came, because he was a few years younger and far more beautiful than she was. And pretty girls she knew had sometimes leaned close to her in the coffee shop. Their breasts had brushed against her arm (their hair smelled of herbs or almonds or vinegar) and they told her, confidentially, how they longed for him.

But at a party at the LSE he reached out and stroked her throat. She looked at the light hanging in his long, black hair and he went home with her that night.

When she woke up the next morning, his face looked childish and swollen in sleep. The hair lay in strings on the pillow. She washed herself all over and dressed in clothes that made her feel tough: black shirt, boots, jeans and a headscarf. She threw the window open, lit a cigarette, sat on the windowsill and turned the radio on full blast. He woke up with a start, sat up in bed and squinted at her from under thick, sticky lids. His face was oily.

The wind ruffled her headscarf. She took another drag of her cigarette. He buried his face in the pillow.

She saw in him sometimes the same thing she saw in all men. An emotional amputation. She could never predict when his feelings would begin or end. And when there was no feeling where she expected to find feeling, it was like a kick in the head. At first she was just irritated. She would screw up her face scornfully and dust off the muck that the boot had left in her hair saying 'Lay off. Lay off my head.' But later it would start to bleed. Not flowing in a healthy stream to be licked off, like tears, but bruising, seeping in a purple puddle under the skin, spreading slowly from the heelmark of her left temple.

Every night she would climb into bed beside him. He would always start by stroking her cheek and she wished he wouldn't because the skin was dry and gritty there. Then she would feel his lip softly and wetly on her eye-lid and she would feel a brimming in her throat, her chest seemed to float up and her nipples prickled at the first touch of his body. He would kiss her neck and chest and still she was aware of how bony her chest was, very conscious of the three or four dark hairs between her breasts. And as he started moving (and she started to admire how he moved), the black hair brushing her cheeks and shoulders, a rush of thoughts and feelings bubbled and boiled in the dark crevices of her mouth. But always, at those moments something would happen, she would lose it, the thoughts and feelings would evaporate painfully from the surface of her teeth and she felt herself becoming more and more transparent as he became more and more tangible reality. And when he was asleep, she would lie on her side, rubbing the softness of her own breast and feeling like a eunuch.

Stubbing the cigarette out in the ashtray by the door, she looked over at his sleeping body. 'If you gave a damn you'd wake up,' she thought but he didn't move so she closed the door quietly behind her.

At nine-thirty the bookshop opened. She sat behind the cash register and read. The other clerk was an eager little bitch who scurried around unnerving shoplifters and chastising little kids with chocolatey fingers. The people who came in were mostly students: long haired men in greatcoats who looked unshaven by the Russian literature, girls wearing high-heeled shoes, in profile by the Dada and Surrealism. Sometimes a dishevelled and odd-smelling professor emerged from the second-hand book room and blinked at the light. Small boys came in and smoked cigarettes by the dirty novels.

Sally was chanting as she came down the stairs, one at a time, on her ass,

> *'Curly locks, curly locks, wilt thou be mine?*
> *Thou shalt not wash dishes, nor yet feed the swine,*
> *But sit on a cushion and sew a fine seam*
> *And feed upon strawberries, sugar and cream.'*

Between the frets of the banister she could see her sister, Janet. Mother was squeezing her into the white lace wedding dress for which she had intended to lose five pounds. Cousins and florists minced around the living room, arranging spring flowers and polishing sideboards. Everyone ignored Sally.

As the orange juice gurgled into a tall glass, Mother came into the kitchen to find a safety pin. 'Get out of those awful pyjamas, darling, and try to look nice. How about that dress I got you last birthday? The floaty one? And put your hair up. Take some of my perfume. Try to look good for your sister's wedding, okay, honey?'

The orange juice looked green around the edges by the light of the fluorescent strip. As she took it upstairs, Sally noticed that everything in the living room (the cushions, the table cloths, the pubescent bride's maid picking her nose in the corner) was lavender and egg-shell yellow.

'I'm going to get drunk as a skunk,' she muttered as she put on jeans and a cotton kurtah. She couldn't really wear her sneakers. 'I can't really wear my sneakers,' she said as she rummaged in the bottom of her mother's closet.

She imagined Jewish weddings. Late at night, under a canopy, with the bride breathing quickly behind a veil that made her complexion look misty. That might be quite enchanting. In that setting, one might be moved to sniff. But a wedding in an Episcopalian church in Westport, where the new crop of pimples on the groom's forehead are all the more noticeable for the morning sunlight, where you can see every grain of face powder on your Aunt Sylvia's nose. 'As a skunk!' she muttered again as the bride moved slowly down the aisle.

The tendons in her soft white neck stood out alarmingly. 'Can she still be holding her breath?' Sally wondered as the organ's sound faded and the street noises could be heard again.

The French windows in the living room were flung open and guests wandered through them after collecting their drinks and hors d'oeuvres. The lawn was sprinkled with fashionable girls. Their lips gleamed fruitily.

Sally pushed her way to the bar, where she picked up a scotch and water and a cutting remark from her mother. 'You could have dressed up just this once. Never give an inch, do you?' The eyes were narrowed before they broke into a smile for a passing in-law.

Sally stepped through the French windows and tried to concentrate on the sky as she crossed the lawn.

Jessie stood on line in the coffee shop for lunch. Arnold sat drinking frothy coffee from a pyrex cup, in the corner booth. Sunlight streamed in through and lit up the left side of his face. When she sat down opposite him, the light made her squint. She hated him to look at her when he hadn't seen her for a while. She was afraid he would discover the asymmetry of her face as she rediscovered the beauty of his. Every time she saw him as a stranger might see him, in the street or the coffee shop (the sunlight shone through his cornea and his left eye burned bright blue), she was amazed. 'I live with that man!' she thought.

As she walked over to the table, carefully, with a plate of sandwiches in one hand and a cup of coffee in the other, he watched how unsteady the cup was. When she sat down, she looked embarrassed, as she often did. She squinted, then blinked, then opened her eyes wide. Her iris constricted. The right eye shone bright green.

'I wish you'd wake me in the mornings,' he said.

'You'd wake up if you wanted to. Besides, you may as well get a few more hours if you can.'

'But I do want to and I don't wake unless I'm woken.'

'Okay,' she said, slipping her knife into the soft, white bread.

She could feel the tension coming, as it did when they spoke sometimes, from nowhere, for no reason. He stared at her eyelids. She looked at her sandwich.

'Why do I suddenly feel as if I've said something wrong?' he said. Kick. She cut the sandwich the other way. It was ridiculous. No one under forty cuts sandwiches into quarters.

They ate in silence for a long time. She wanted to talk about silly things. When they did that (over beer or in the park or the time he sneaked into her room at his parents' house) she felt quite close to him. At one point she glanced up at him and smiled. He smiled back and stroked her wrist. She felt things were better now. Better than they had been for some time. She felt something inside her peel and part, like an orange, and lie there, fresh and wet and newly exposed. She would talk, tell him something funny.

'A peculiar old man came into the shop today,' she began. But when she looked up she could see he was impermeable. He was stirring his coffee though he didn't take sugar.

'I don't want just to let it go,' he said. He was watching the bubbles go round and round on the coffee. Occasionally he looked up. Then back at his coffee. 'I sometimes feel we're still living together because you can't be bothered to tell me to leave.'

Reluctantly she let go of the peculiar old man story.

'No,' she said slowly, 'but I think it started mainly because I felt flattered ... that someone like you ... ' She looked up. A worried smile flickered across her face. The way he looked frightened her. She thought for a moment the centre of her had caved in.

'Well, I'll move out then,' he said. He kept looking from one of her eyes to the other. His face seemed different. Not beautiful. Not composed. Coffee was dribbling down his chin. She felt embarrassed looking at him. 'If that's it then,' he went on, 'if you don't ... ' He stood up quickly, making her start. He put his coat on and wiped his chin on the sleeve as he did so. She felt strangely unmoved as she watched him leave, almost running, his black hair streaming down his back, his shoulders bent toward the door.

By mid-afternoon the champagne had run out. Janet had changed into a primrose yellow dress and jacket. She wore a picture hat with two ostrich feathers and a linen rose on it. She laughed a lot. Uncle Sidney drove them to the airport in his Cadillac. Mother had shredded a dozen roses so that everyone could throw petals.

Sally's cheerleader cousin Tracy followed her to see Janet off, to the bar and back to the garden table. She babbled constantly. Sally watched the relatives reeling by. The paunchy, red-faced uncles fingering the asses of Janet's college friends. The litter on the lawn. Hors d'oeuvres trodden into the grass. There was a woman sitting alone at the table behind Tracy. Sally hadn't noticed her before. The woman's face was pale and oval. She had a high forehead and light brown hair, threaded with grey, which flowed down to the small of her back. Her cheekbones and browbones were distinctly carved and her eyes were deep-set between them. She must have been thirty-three or so. Tracy put her hands behind her neck. (Her voice still babbled in the background.) The woman's face was framed in the triangle made by Tracy's bent arm and her head. For a moment the woman looked up and straight into Sally's eyes. Her iris was a bright, pale blue. The pupils were pinpoints. Then eyelids again as she looked away.

Tracy tilted her head into the triangle. 'Are you listening to me?'

'Of course. Go on.'

An executive type, tall with thick, grey hair, walked up to the woman. She stood up and took his arm. They walked across the lawn. She was carrying a fur coat. It was trailing on the lawn behind her. She was tonguing the man's ear as they meandered over the grass. Sally knocked her glass over. The gin flowed over the table and dripped into the grass.

Sally got up and went for another drink, leaving her cousin in mid-sentence. She had mixed drinks. She had had a lot of champagne. Walking was surprisingly difficult. A friend of her mother's who had flat feet and bad breath intercepted her to make some lame comment about the younger daughter's getting married first. As she stumbled past him, he was asking if she was a liberated woman. Once through the French windows, she walked straight into her mother, who said in a voice of overdramatised disgust, 'You're drunk!'

The crowd at the bar was too much to handle and Sally could feel a smarting around the edges of her eyes. If she cried at her sister's wedding, on top of everything else, she would never hear the last of it from her mother, so she stumbled past the crowd and up the stairs to her room. She locked the door and lay down on the bed. Her cheeks were wet. The saliva in her mouth was hot. She put one hand behind her head and the other down the front of her jeans. Every few seconds the sound of hysterical feminine laughter dribbled in through the crack in the window. Tears were winding into her ears and the corners of her mouth. She started to move her pelvis back and forth. Three fingers lay against the wet opening of her vagina. The fourth rubbed rhythmically on her clitoris. Again the screeching laughter from outside and the light from the window blurred and spangled in the film of water on her eyes. Her shoes fell onto the floor. Her toes pointed till they touched the bed. When her orgasm started she bent her knee and raised her body up, arching her back. The spasm ran to the bones in her ankles and the roots of her hair.

Jessie arrived ten minutes late from lunch. The sun on the display window showed exactly how the man had washed it the day before. First up and down, then back and forth, then round and round as he got disgruntled toward the end.

She sat behind the cash register reading *Dubliners*. Periodically she paused to gauge what she was feeling. She felt a little guilty for feeling nothing but the sun on her face and Joyce's words tumbling slowly through her mind. That afternoon most of the customers were just looking. She smiled at more of them than she usually did.

At six o'clock she stepped out into the wind. There were few people on the street and the sky was a very deep blue. As she walked toward the flat she felt as though she were waiting for herself to say something. When she reached the building, she looked up at her bedroom window. There was no sign of movement.

Nadia Wheatley

An Unwritten Story:
Explanation of (Plus Apology for)

The Setting
This is the Author. Watch her sweep.

Swish-swish, swish-swish, what a lovely sound. Soon she'll
have the dirt from all the corners and crannies in a nice little
pile in the centre of the room, and then Flip-whoosh, Flip-
whoosh, she'll sweep the dirt with the small brush into the pink
plastic dustpan and the whole floor will sparkle and shine.
Well, not quite, for it really needs a mop too, but she is
contenting herself with merely sweeping today, mopping
tomorrow. After all she's an Author, not a bloody housewife.

The Author looks up now. She smiles apologetically. She is
very sorry that she hasn't written a story for you today. There
was a story that she was going to make for you today, a real
story with words, grammar, syntax, language, plus characters
even, a plot, conversation, action, a theme, analysis, *feeling*,
and a moral to boot; but somehow, the sweeping, it gets
behind until you simply cannot put it off another moment; you
know how it is. She would have loved to have given the story to
you. It is a pity isn't it. Never mind.

192

The Setting (*again, folks*)

This is the Author: watch.

We call her the Author although she is a female person because she hates the word 'Authoress'. (She's liberated.) We call her the Author because we prefer to be polite to her; after all, she is polite to us.

You can tell that this Author is a female person because she wears an apron. This is not an infallible test, I admit; it is true that certain male persons wear aprons — butchers, for example, and chefs and sometimes carpenters and of course Masons and husbands cooking the picnic barbecue. But in a case such as this where it is known that the wearer is an Author it is a reliable test, for male-Authoring is not one of the occupations in which aprons are used. The Author wears her apron for writing as well as sweeping: that way she can pop in and out between paragraphs and salt the potatoes. Most eaters prefer salt in their potatoes. The people who wear the Author's potatoes are no exception.

Change of Scene

Let's have a change of scene now shall we? After all, an Author(ess) is not an inexhaustible topic. Shall we look at a man instead?

This is a Man. He lives in the same house as the Author. Ooooooh look, here's another one! He does too. They are not sweeping. (They read.) Though they do sweep sometimes, mind you. These are not sexist Men. You'd be surprised to see how often it happens that after the Author has swept around the house for about half an hour 'doing a Shulamith Firestone' the Men too take up Squeegees, dustpans, damp rubber sponges, New Ajax. It's pretty easy to prey on their conscience. They have read even more Greer-Mitchell-Firestone-Millet-etc. than the Author has; they are very fast readers (because, being male, they are intelligent?). Also, at night, when the three of them read, she often has to keep one eye on the potatoes. These Men like salt on their spuds.

The phrase 'doing a Shulamith Firestone' is a household

in-joke. (It is a witty and literate household, so there are jokes.)
The Author made up the joke. (She isn't one of those feminists
who have lost their sense of humour.) One day, when she was
very angry, sweeping, her face set, feeling martyr-ish, hating
all men, the Men started getting nervous. The Author sensed
this (because, being female, she is sensitive?) and felt guilty. Oh
don't mind me, she said, (or words to this effect), I am just
sweeping because I feel like it, don't think I'm doing a
Shulamith Firestone. (Sorry, I guess it's one of those jokes that
don't repeat very well, but it certain caused a laugh at the time
and relieved the tension.) The Men took over the joke. So now
when the Author silently sweeps and her mouth takes on a
Buchenwald look the Men nudge each other and smile and say,
Oh look, she's doing a Shulamith Firestone. The words 'Shulamith Firestone' have also become in this household a synonym
for what unliberated women call 'the chores'. The Author has
forgotten (because, being female, she is scatterbrained?) that
this was originally her 'joke'.

A Spot of Action: a Story Even
Enough scene-setting. Let's have a bit of action now, a story
even. That's what you came for isn't it?

A woman (the Author) sweeps. She has a nice little pile of
dirt in the middle of the room. It is growing. Swish-swish. Her
face is very set and red and she looks angry and most
unattractive. Her hair is pulled back with elastic. You cannot
hear what she is saying because she is speaking to herself inside
her head. Her words, if you want to know (and I apologise
because they are so dull, but she is not being clever, witty,
original, whatever, because after all the Men cannot hear the
words inside her head), these words are along the lines of
Bloody Men, fucking *men*, it's all very well them offering to do
the washing-up, they never even *see* the dirt in the corners, I've
never known a man who defrosted a fridge or cleaned a bath
off his own bat, why didn't their mothers ever teach them, I've
left that bottle-top there on the step for a *week* now and they
haven't even noticed it, they're not even offering today, just

sitting on their arses reading. Her head is also plotting the disgusting jobs she will set them in revenge when finally they notice she is sweeping and come in to say: Is there another broom.

The Plot Thickens

You must be getting sick of this Beckettish one-actor stuff, so:

Enter: A Man (one of the two we saw before).

He opens his mouth. He speaks. The Author knows what he will say (because, being female, she is intuitive?). He will say: Is there another broom.

Dialogue

The Man opens his mouth. He speaks. The Author was wrong (because she is female?). The man does not say: Is there another broom. He says: I have just been reading your latest short story. It's marvellous, absolutely superb! I am quite bowled over by it! You really get to grips with that housewife, whatshername, and with the sort of liberated studenty woman too; but no, really, *all* your female characters are marvellously done. And the way you capture the rhythms of women's thoughts! Absolutely superb! I simply couldn't put it down. And your analysis of the role-playing in this sexist society: quite fantastic! I'd really like to talk to you about it some time. By the way, is there another broom.

The Author's face flushes redder: happy red. Exhilarated red. Joy. Praise. Recognition. We see that she's really not ugly at all.

Oh no, she says, no really, no truly, no I'm only doing this because I feel like a break. Swish-swish.

Action

The Man departs. (We do not see the other man.)

The Ending (*always the most important part to a story I think, don't you?*)

A woman approaches me. It is the Author.

She whispers in my ear. She tells me that she would like me to apologise to you for the fact that she did not write a story for you today but really, really-truly (she whispers sincerely), really it was one of those days when she just felt like a break. You know how it is.

Frances Landsman

Tampax

you can swim in tampax
you can ride
and sail
and more,
even if you couldn't do
any of these things before

Frustruation

do you struate?
a little girl
asked my youngest son
no, he said
not me, he said
it doesn't sound like fun
it's not, she said
it's not at all
it hurts like hell below
s'pose that's why only men struate, he said
with a proud brave manly glow

Advice

he said no other
could be wiser
and offered me the job
of sexual adviser
but when he discovered
i really knew better
he said ...
when i want your fucking advice i'll ask for it

Eileen Fairweather

Sacrifice
(*extract from a novel in progress*)

When first her breasts started to grow she had been sick with fear and shame; why couldn't she stay a child, she did not want to be a woman.

The dusty book on top of Mum's wardrobe said that only girls with impure thoughts developed early, and she was only twelve, but already rounded. For nearly a year, day in and day out, she had secretly worn last year's tight constricting swimsuit beneath her vest, her thighs rubbed raw and having to totally undress each time for the toilet, but she was desperate to be flattened.

The hairs sprouting down there she removed with nail scissors.

When her period finally began, December the 7th, 1966, she had cried every night for a week, feeling humiliated and dirty as her mother had whispered about 'monthlies' and shown her where to hide the STs.

At school the nuns gave them a book, *Now You're Growing Up*, telling how she would have to wash down there, especially those times, but always with her eyes shut, and praying to the

Blessed Virgin, to guard against the wicked thoughts. But she had to look a little — water splashed all over the floor otherwise, and Mum would be cross. When she looked, sure enough the thought came, the man putting his thingie into your mouth and peeing, it had to be that, well what other opening did a woman have? The thought disgusted her. Drying herself she realised that she'd thought the wicked thing, so she said an Act of Contrition, this time with her eyes firmly closed.

The book also talked of how blessed and wonderful were motherhood and married life, they were the best things a woman could do, that or be a nun.

Bridget thought she might be a nun.

A star had beamed straight at her one night, and she knew then that she had been chosen for a saint, so she had better be a nun, because whoever heard of a saint being married. Saint Thomas More had been, but then he was a man.

Lady saints were always Virgin Martyrs, with pretty lilies to show they had died pure.

At night, in bed, she practised burning herself with the hot water bottle, so she would be ready when the torture came.

The Feast of the Holy Family, January 8th that was, again Dad managed to drag Mum with them to the Church; he wasn't going to see her Lapse again, and so soon after Christmas. And the children had been glad, it was a dreadful thing to have a Lapsed Catholic for a mother, but they were miserable too, because they knew she was terrified of the Church — the roof would collapse on her, she had cried. When finally she fainted they had dragged her out, red in the face and Dad already cursing, oh you sick and wicked woman, while the priest continued with her sermon on the sanctity of family life, pretending not to have noticed them.

While Mum was in the hospital the four sisters had to fend for themselves — he was doing overtime he said, did they know how much they cost to keep? — but they did not mind, his temper was so bad. Mrs Bell from next door helped with the new baby, and they told their friends at school that Mum was away looking after a sick aunt.

Late at night he would creep into their bedroom, shout it was their fault that Mum was in the nut-house, disobedient lazy sluts that they were, oh you're your mother's daughters all right he would say.

Then they would make resolutions to be better behaved, plot strategies on how they'd help her, and end by throwing insults and blame, no it's *you* who's the laziest. Kathy and Teresa ganging up against her, calling her Snob, Squint-Eyes, because she went to the Grammar School.

Well they were stupid, only cared about boys, what did they know. One day she'd be famous, because she was clever, then they'd see. Or a saint. But she never told them that one.

One thing they all agreed on was that they were never, ever going to get married.

Eventually Mum came back, and went to work, the doctor had said it would do her good. Two years she stayed at the fish and chip shop, but Bridget never told anyone; at school they thought her common enough as it was, with her father working in the prison. Once she told a new girl he was the Governor, when really he was just an ordinary warder. She was soon found out though, and then how they teased her. One day Sister Bonaventure told her off in class, 'Bridget, you sound just like a Cockney, it is not "walkin" but "walk*ing*", with a g — remember?' and she felt a bright blush of shame, the same as when her father had yelled at her, 'We're working class, Madam Mighty, and you bloody well remember that, we don't want none of your Convent school mannerisms brung home here.'

Because she didn't want to be working class, because being working class meant cups without saucers, and bottles of milk on the table — he'd yelled at her because he'd caught her putting it into a jug — and watching Coronation Street and reading the News of the World, all the things Sister Imelda found so shocking when Bridget filled in the Family Pastimes class questionnaire.

Being working class meant you were stupid and lazy, because it was true God rewarded those who helped themselves, well look at John F Kennedy. And anyway, it was so unfair of him to go on at her like that, after all it was he who had been so desperate for her to get to St Xavier's. Hadn't he always said that she got her brains from him, and that this time they weren't going to be wasted; she wasn't going to have to leave no village school at 14, even if he had.

But now she was 14 and already he was demanding that she get off her fat arse and earn some money — yes, find out what the *real* world is like, Miss High and Mighty — she could be a typist or work in a shop, learn to make do the way her sisters had.

The very thought terrified her, she would die in that world, she knew that just from working in the hairdressers. She had been there a year, Saturdays and two nights a week after school, because he was damned if he was going to pay pocket money for her to go tart herself up. 'We've got four children in this family already, Madam, and that's quite enough,' he had said. Her mother had gone pale at that, and Bridget knew then that she was thinking of Kathy who had run all the way to America after her soldier, except he was nowhere to be found and so she stuck up a knitting needle instead.

The hospital chaplain had written to Mum, at one point he'd had to give Kath the Last Rites, but somehow she had pulled through. Dad wasn't to know though, he'd kill her if he knew, because abortion was murder.

One day at the hairdressers Bett, one of the stylists, collapsed while doing a customer, blood trickling down her leg. In the ant-ridden back-room all the girls shut up when Bridget came in, nothing to fuss about they said, it was only a bad period. Not long afterwards Bridget had admired Bett's new coat, but wasn't £30 a lot of money? and Bett had laughed bitterly, what was 30 quid when she'd just spent 50 on nothing?

And then Bridget understood that this was the same thing as Kathy had done, and realised that either she, personally, knew two murderers, or that the Church was wrong. Because surely Bett and Kathy had only ever hurt themselves. They were good girls really.

At the hairdressers the girls talked incessantly about

202

make-up and men and clothes, and how glad they would be to get married and escape from work, while the factory women having the purple tints talked on and on about how awful their husbands were. While Bridget just listened, feeling nervous and prim and out of place. But one thing was sure, she wasn't going to be like them, or like her sisters, she was going to grow up beautiful and very clever, and marry a poet.

Other times she would graciously grant interviews to the mirror in her parents' bedroom, explaining how she managed to combine being first woman Prime Minister with having ten children. She was sure it was possible, because she wanted it to be.

She wanted to have everything, not like these women who only had their weekly hair-dos to look forward to, and who only talked with animation when discussing last night's Hughie Green, wasn't he a laugh?

For the purposes of the hairdressers she had reverted back to Cockney. She did not like to feel out of place.

And always in between was the realisation that God wanted her for a nun — He had sent her signs in so many ways. The nuns thought so too, and they encouraged her to go on with the Retreats and the all-night vigils, where she would pray to her loving Christ. He alone could save her from the fantasies stirred up by Mick Jagger.

Once, while she was doing the Stations of the Cross, the headmistress, Mother Mary Matthew, came up silently behind her and started tugging at her skirt; her devotion was very touching, she hissed, but the shortness of her skirts was not. Bridget could not even imagine explaining how the skirt was a cast-off from Teresa, who was shorter and slimmer. She wanted to run away and cry, but forced herself to continue the twelve-station round, her face bright crimson as she imagined the eyes of the whole church upon her. In the end she realised that her anger was wrong and ungrateful, for the humiliation was in fact a gift from Christ, to save her from the sin of pride, into which she was always falling; the times she thought herself clever, or when someone said something nice about her and she let herself feel pleased.

She thought she would be a social worker nun, and do good for others less fortunate than herself, seeing as God had granted her so many blessings — her faith, the nuns, her family, her intelligence and such a good school. Sometimes she would cry for hours, unsure as to why, perhaps it was because she was so happy; Christ, He loved her so much, and she Him!

Although it was true that she had achieved nothing at all in bettering things between her own parents. And maybe her father was right when he yelled at her that Charity should begin at home! the time he caught her giving to the Missions when she should have been saving for the shoes; he was damned if he would pay. How dare she play the do-gooder while he scrimped and scraped 'all so you can fill your head with nonsense when you'll only go off and get married and waste it all!'

Of course, he was very proud of her really.

At school she was getting into trouble, her work was falling off and nowadays she was always late. But it was so difficult to wake when she'd been up half the night, trying to keep Mum's hand from the bottle and keeping her company till Dad finally fell asleep, and it was safe for her to join him. 'He's told you he leads the life of a monk, Bridget,' she would slur, in her thickening Glasgow accent, 'but no monk has ever had it away as much as he has. Well, God bless the Holy Mother Church! — come on, Bridget, let's toast the Church eh, you can do it with tea seeing as you're so young — and good luck to the Virgin Mary! Long may she stay that way — the frigid old cow. Ah, but it's the only way for a woman to be, Bridget, you take it from your Mamma.'

Bridget would listen in pity and horror, praying to God to forgive her, Mum didn't mean it really. Till at last her mother would collapse head first on the table, spittle oozing from her mouth as she cried her nightly lullaby, but you're only a baby, Bridget, I've no right to tell you of these things, but I've no-one else to talk to, Bridget, no-one, no-one.

And Bridget would try not to cry, she had to be strong for both of them, make up to Mummy for never having had a

204

Mum of her own — hers had died giving birth to her — make up to her for having a husband like — but no, she mustn't think like that, it was ungrateful and wicked.

One night she had to call him down, Mum having collapsed on the floor and Bridget not strong enough to lift her. He scooped her up like she was an injured dog in some gutter, bloody and disgusting, but then doesn't a warder always do his duty. And suddenly Mum regained consciousness, and was laughing at him, still slurring but somehow very lucid as she spat: 'You think you're going to have me now, don't you, you sex-mad bastard? But you'll never have me again the way you want me, oh no siree, because I'll have you know that I've been taking ... the pill! See,' she giggled, triumphant, into his face, 'I'm a wha'd'-ye-call-it, a liberated woman now, and you can have me every night or you can poke the fire with it for all I care, but you'll never get me that way again!'

And for once it was his turn to look frightened, for she was like a witch, mad and vicious to the very last flame, high on anger and hate and therefore beyond their torture, beyond their power.

So all he managed was some muttering about the mad drunken Irish, at which she struggled free, and stood, swaying, against the sink, her finger stabbing at him: 'Yes I am Irish! And I'm proud of it!' which both surprised and shocked Bridget, because normally she claimed to be Scots, 'Aye, a Scot I am, and loyal to the Queen!' But then she remembered another night her mother had over-drunk when Kevin and Rose had come with their thick brogues, and their memories of her early childhood, getting her tiddly to the point where she had switched from Scotland the Brave to things called Rebel songs, about potatoes and killings. 'Well yes,' she had joked, while Dad sat looking tight-lipped and left-out, 'maybe I am Irish, even if you are all a load of drunken rogues and liars — because don't think I've forgot my father, though God knows at least *he* was a laugh.' But being Irish was like being working class, and Bridget didn't like to think of it.

Her mother was shouting now, 'And if I am drunk and mad

it's because you've made me that way, you with your swearings and beatings and cursing, you the holy one who's throwing your fists around the minute you're off the church steps.' And then she stepped up close to him, while he backed away, white and shaken because he had never seen her this way before. 'Yes, sir,' she hissed, 'it's you who's killed religion for me, it's you and your hypocrisy have robbed me of the faith I was born with — you pious bloody convert! And then you *dare* try turn my own children from me — oh, I know the poison you're pouring in their ears when you're off at Mass, Mr Holy Joe — my own children, you bastard!'

And then she hit at him with her small shaking fists, till Bridget's sobs and pullings reminded her of the daughter's presence; 'What are you doing still up?' she muttered.

'Come to bed Mum — *please*,' but she pushed Bridget away, clinging for support to a chair instead. 'Oh Breege, Breege,' she said softly. 'It's no use. But don't think I was always like this, don't think I didn't have fight in me once. Because I did. It's in my blood, lovey — or was, till he sucked it all away. Like my parents —' and she stopped, forgetting what it was she had to say; 'yes, my parents ... now they knew what real faith was, fought for it, they did — and their country. Not like him — religion just another stick to beat you over the head with.'

Her loose-hanging smile fell away; 'Up the IRA,' she said weakly. Then she saw the terror in Bridget's eyes, Sweet Jesus, don't let it be true, not again, oh not *my* Mum! and laughed.

'Ah, don't you look so shocked, Bridget,' she said, wheeling round and grabbing the girl, dribbling into her ear, 'No, you haven't much to be proud of with your family, have ye darlin', but rather be proud of mine than your father's lot, because a meaner tight-fisted cold lot of bastards you couldn't meet — and those that were too short for the Army joined the Black and Tans. Well — at least it kept them off the streets!' and she laughed uproariously at her own joke.

Then she put her arm around the child, peering at her in amusement and distaste; 'But don't let it worry you that of all my kids it's you who's the spit image of your dad, it's not your fault, and you may grow out of it yet. And you'll get your schooling, if it's over my dead body — and more than likely it will be,' she had said, shooting a look of pure hate at the father, 'because why else do you think I let that pig paw at my body if not to stop him getting at yous. No, you'll get your chance my little darlin', and it will be no thanks to your father, though sure as hell he'll want the credit for it. So when your mother's old and a drunkard, don't you forget that it was her gave you your chance, paid for it night in and night out with her body and her bruises. The same as my mother would have done for me if my father hadn't killed her first, the way they always kill you.'

And then she stumbled into the centre of the room, speaking as though to a huge meeting, crying and giggling at the same time as she screamed 'And look what my brave brave parents fought for! To "liberate" me to an English fucking screw ... oh, aye, a screw!'

And then again she collapsed, this time into a total unconsciousness, Bridget sobbing into her father's arms, for the first time consciously hating him, but needing him, God never listened anyway so Daddy Daddy what are we going to do? And he patting her, sssh, long suffering, I can see it will have to be the hospital again for *her*.

Anya Bostock

In the Shit No More
a true story

The first thought that occurs to me as I start telling this story is: they'll say I'm a fool, spoilt, privileged, pretentious and moralising.

I've been in Women's Liberation for nearly four years and the 'they' in my last sentence are other women. That tells you something for a start, about the movement or women in general or just about me, I'm not sure.

OK, think what you like, I'll tell it anyway. It only happened last weekend. But you'll have to know some facts about me first.

I'm fifty-one years old, I'm self-supporting and always have been, I've brought up children and lived with men. The last of my men left a year ago. He was the one I cared about longest and when he left, it hurt. I'm getting over it, now.

When I say I'm self-supporting it's true in the sense that I've always earned a reasonably good living, working at a desk. And I can cook and housekeep adequately (my children are healthy, which proves it I suppose) but not what you might call well. I can't make dresses and my cakes come out damp in the centre. When I lay the table, somebody (usually me) has to get up at least three times because something's missing.

So long as there as a man (and until a year ago there always was a man) those were the kind of shortcomings I was aware of in myself and used to worry about. You're a failure as a woman, I told myself on many occasions.

Since the man left, I've come to think that making dresses and cakes is maybe not all that important. Anyway I wouldn't have the time. It's amazing how busy it keeps you, being sole breadwinner and adult in a family of three.

What worries me nowadays is that I haven't a clue about how to do any of the man-type things (other than being the breadwinner, I mean). Electrical jobs, household repairs, putting up shelves — I've suddenly realised that I just never have done any one of those things. Lots of women do them, I know, but I've always been a Mary not a Martha, and quite smug about it.

Which brings me to last weekend.

The lavatory seat in my flat is a black plastic job with a lid. The lid broke when we moved in eighteen months ago and the man stood on it to fix the light. He was going to replace it, only he left.

On Saturday afternoon I couldn't go out as I usually try to do (we live near the country and I like to walk) because my kids were home, sick. One had 'flu and the other was recovering after an accident. So I said to myself, right, you're going to do the ironing (piled up for a month) and you're also going to replace the lavatory seat. I bought a new one at the super-market.

First I couldn't discover how or where the thing was fixed on. I pulled at the seat a bit and it wouldn't budge and I was no wiser than before. I asked Marcelline who lives upstairs. There's a flat bit behind the pan, she said, feel underneath and you'll find two screws. I did. They were quite hefty screws with wing nuts and the wing nuts wouldn't turn. Also, as soon as I touched them I got this brown stuff on my fingers. Rust, I thought, but it wasn't, it was shit.

As soon as I realised this I couldn't any longer do what I was already feeling tempted to do, namely, forget about the whole thing. Exposed shit in your lavatory is intolerable, it's part of being a failure as a woman, you can't just leave it there nor can you ask someone else to deal with it except perhaps your man if you happen to be on very good terms with him. I suppose I wouldn't be ashamed to tell the other women in my group about the exposed and ancient shit in my lavatory, but I would certainly not ask them to help me to remove it, they've enough troubles of their own. I had to do it myself. There was nothing else for it.

The lavatory is quite narrow and I'm a large woman. I knelt down and tried to get a grip on the nearest wing nut, wrapping a piece of rag round it. No good. I wiped my hands on the rag and went to look in the toolbox. It was in a mess and none of the tools in it looked as if they'd be any use.

In my work I deal with words. I know a lot of words, a lot of nouns and generally I know how to use them, but my idea of what objects those nouns actually represent is often vague. Gazing into the chaos of the toolbox I realised that, with the exception of hammer, screw-driver, saw and a very few others, I could not match any of the tool words I knew with the tools in the box, still less with the one which wasn't there and which I thought would probably do the trick. Are pliers this ⟨drawing⟩ or this ⟨drawing⟩? And is this ⟨drawing⟩ a wrench? If so, I needed a wrench. By going back to the supermarket I'd avoid the embarrassment of having to ask. I went back to the supermarket (luckily it's next door to our block of flats), chose a ⟨drawing⟩ that looked strong enough, and also bought a small can of machine oil. The ⟨drawing⟩ had a hole at the end of its handle. I would put the screwdriver in the hole and twist it.

Back in the flat I filled a plastic bowl with water, found a few more rags, pushed up the sleeves of my sweater and set to work.

First I washed the screw with a rag soaked in water (a surprising amount of shit came away), then I squirted oil into it, then I fixed the — let's call it wrench to save time, even if it isn't — on to the wing of the nearest nut, then I thrust the screwdriver through the hole and began to push. The nut turned a tiny little bit, then jammed again. The wrench slipped off.

I repeated the process over and over again, and some of the times the nut turned a little. But because I had to keep reapplying the wrench, and the screwdriver was never in the same position as before, and I couldn't get my head near enough to see because of lack of space, I was never sure in which direction I ought to twist the screwdriver: I twisted it in a clockwise direction until it wouldn't turn any further, then back again as far as it would go, cursing myself for a fool, dropping this and that, going to fetch yet more rags, changing the water in the plastic bowl, getting very dirty and hot. All this was taking a long time, and the smell was strong.

The children came to the door and said, what on earth are you doing. Don't ask, I said, I'll tell you later, go away, please. They went back to bed.

After a while I thought I'd give that side a rest, and tried the other. Disconcertingly, this wing nut yielded quite soon. This is where I made my big mistake. Heady with success, I unscrewed the nut, pulled out the long screw which went through the hole in the flat bit behind the pan (larger pieces of shit than before, mixed with water and oil, fell on the floor and spattered the wall), and rattled again at the lavatory seat. To my surprise it came away almost at once.

Triumph? Yes, in a way. But the first screw was still there, with only a small, flat, square piece at the top. Now that the seat was no longer there to keep the screw from turning, I suddenly needed four hands. I only had two, covered in shit, slippery with oil and sore with twisting.

Ask one of the children for help? Just to put a pair of pliers (if they are pliers) on that flat square piece and immobilise the screw?

Why not?

Well, two reasons. One rational (they wouldn't like the shit), the other not. By now it had become extremely important that I should do this job entirely by myself, from start to finish.

I am a person who lives by anticipation. I am full of fears

because I anticipate bad things, and this is a weakness. But I also have quite a developed capacity for anticipating good things ('looking forward') and this I know is a strength. Now that my life is not very safe or cosy and I have to clutch at straws, I try to make the most of this capacity, this strength. And I had certainly begun to look forward to the satisfaction I would feel if I finished this filthy job all by myself.

So. I fitted the wrench on the flat piece at the top of the screw, gripped it in my left hand, wrapped the rag round the nut and very slowly, with the fingers of my sore, aching right hand, began to twist it this way and that, for I was still not sure which direction was the right one.

It took hours, literally. Stopping from time to time to squirt in more oil (surely I used far too much oil but I had become superstitious about it; oil was my only friend). And in the end it was done.

But I would not allow myself to feel elated until I had washed everything down (the holes through which the pins went were encrusted with shit, I wrapped the screwdriver in yet another wet rag and jabbed it in and pulled it out, again and again), washed and disinfected the plastic bowl, scrubbed my hands, fitted on the new seat, taken off all my clothes and put them in the washing machine, washed my arms up to the shoulder, scrubbed my hands again and put hand cream on them, and dressed in clean clothes.

My Saturday afternoon had gone, it was time to think of supper. But first I would pour myself a glass of wine, light a cigarette and savour my elation. I'd done it! I had succeeded in doing something which previously I wouldn't even have attempted. It had turned out ten times more difficult and disgusting than I had imagined, and still I'd gone ahead and done it.

And it had been a man-type job. Cleaning up a small child with diarrhoea is something different. Doing something for another person is woman-type work, doing something to gain a secondary benefit (even like earning a living) is woman-type work. Men, I was taught, grapple with things just for the fun of getting the better of them, they pit themselves against mountains and machinery. My duel with the lavatory seat had been the nearest I'd got to pure sport in fifty-one years. My very own, private Olympiad.

Euphoria was beginning to set in, and I thought of the women in my group who are always warning me (and, I believe, warning themselves through me) against the tendency to euphorise. Some are irritated by it, others tolerate it because they are fond of me, but not one of them shares it. They are afraid euphoria will dilute their sense of purpose.

I know that there's nothing to celebrate about having to do all the woman-type jobs as well as the man-type ones. Liberation is a harsh-tasting fruit if it means sleeping alone, having no one to share your responsibilities or your rare moments of euphoria, racing against the clock all day, never having time to yourself, ageing prematurely, being dismissed by men (and women outside the movement) as a troublemaker, a bore, or, at best, a 'character'.

But, I thought, my dear sisters, I won't let you put me off feeling happy. As I'm not letting your imaginary criticisms stop me now from writing down the story of my battle. There isn't any lesson in what I'm telling you. Anyway I don't believe in lessons taught by one person to another, only in those we deduce ourselves from experience. But experience can 'and should be pooled.

I learned a number of things from that afternoon's experience:

(a) There's no mystery about using tools. Even a clumsy idiot like me can use them.

(b) There are no woman-type jobs or man-type jobs. There is a typical female attitude to work, which consists in minimising any direct enjoyment that can be got out of it and emphasising the indirect satisfaction to be derived from its usefulness; and a typical male attitude, which plays up the gratuitous pleasure ('creativity') for all it's worth and shies away from the secondary ancillary aspect. Both sexes are capable of either attitude, and both attitudes are incomplete.

(c) My real friend in the struggle with the lavatory seat was not the oil, slippery and intrusive like all intermediaries, but the screw itself. I remember how, for a long time, I didn't know which way to turn the nut but kept twisting anyway, in both directions. Little by little the right direction asserted itself until presently the screw which had been there, getting progressively more encrusted ever since the block of flats was built (or since the beginning of time?), came loose and clear.

This is where you all start telling me not to be pretentious. But I'll say it all the same. I know I am not — we are not — out of the shit yet, not by a long way. Half the time we aren't even sure which way to push. But when we get to the end of it — for, like those bloody screws, it does have an end, I'm sure of it — I guarantee you a moment of elation before the next job clamours to be done.

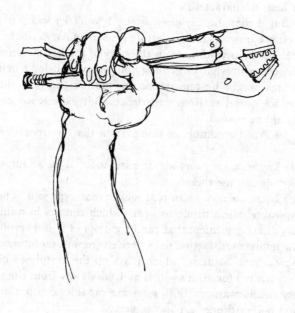

Notes on the Contributors

Lynda Schor lives in New York City and is the author of the collection of short stories *Appetites*. Another volume of stories, *True Love and Real Romance*, will be published in 1979.

Ros Carne was born in London in 1951. She has recently moved to Dublin where she works as a freelance journalist.

Merseyside Women's Literature Collective was a group of five women who came together in 1971 to produce a collection of revamped fairy tales. Two of the stories, 'Red Riding Hood' and 'The Prince and the Swineherd', are being published in pamphlet form by the Moss Side Press, a woman-run printshop in Manchester.

Judith Kazantzis lives with her husband and children in London. 'Things I'll remember when I'm old: having two children, the intense resentment and love, then calmer waters as they grew up; joining my first consciousness-raising group in 1971; having my first book of poetry, *Minefield*, out in 1977.'

Susan Wallbank lives in London with her husband and three daughters and works as a counsellor with 'Cruse', the organisation for widows and their children. With five other women she has produced a collection of poems, *House Plant*, and she has nearly completed a children's story book and a book of verse for children.

Tina Reid was born in the Midlands. She became involved in the Women's Liberation Workshop in London in 1969, and then spent five years living and working in a commune in Scotland. Now she lives with her two children and friends in London and works in a neighbourhood advice centre. Her poetry appears in the collection *Licking the Bed Clean* (1978). She started trying to publish 'because of the encouragement of a very brave Scottish feminist writer, Joan Ure, who is now dead. Read her work if you can find it.'

Amiya Rao was born in India and educated at Oxford. With her husband she has written several books on Indian politics, and she was involved in underground work during the Emergency in India. She lives in New Delhi.

Astra has been involved in the women's liberation movement in London since 1971, for most of that time as a radical feminist. She has been active in the Women's Liberation Literature Collective since 1972, and her work has appeared in the Collective's four anthologies, in *Spare Rib*, and in *Fighting Words*, published by Onlywomen Press. She is a playworker at a Women's Aid refuge, and is currently working on a collection of poems about her mother.

Stef Pixner was born in London in 1945. She teaches sociology and psychology in a London polytechnic and lives with friends in East London. A member of a women writers' group, she has published poetry and drawings in the collectively published *Licking the Bed Clean* (1978).

Ann Oosthuizen lives in London, works at a Women's Aid refuge, and belongs to a women writers' group. She was born in Cape Town, South Africa, married at twenty-one and had three children. She left South Africa for good in 1972; *Bones* is 'an attempt to understand the years leading up to my departure'.

Stephanie Smolensky is 'a compulsive writer and reader, time-waster and tea-brewer. Age thirty-one, has lived in Notting Hill for the past seven years, mainly on the dole. Can be seen most Fridays down Portobello Road market, looking for fair-isle woolies and novels by women authors.'

Gillian Allnutt lives in a squat in London and works at part-time jobs in order to have time to write. She was a member of the prose-writing workshop at the Women's Arts Alliance — 'an invaluable source of critical support' — and still attends the poetry workshop there. She is working on a feminist autobiographical novel.

Marit Paulsen was born in Norway in 1939, and married at seventeen. After her two children were born she went to work in a steel factory and in the years following worked in the fish industry, hotel trade and metal industry. She was active in the metal workers union until a back injury forced her to leave manual work. Since *You, Human Being* she has written five books and worked for the Swedish trade union press.

Angela Hamblin contributed to the first two anthologies produced by the Women's Literature Collective, of which she was a founder member. Her work has also appeared in the anthology *Conditions of Illusion* (Feminist Books), and she compiled and edited *The Other Side of Adoption*. She is currently working on a study of rape.

Fay Weldon's first novel *The Fat Woman's Joke* appeared in 1967. Since then she has published *Down Among the Women*, *Female Friends*, *Little Sisters*, and *Praxis*, and has written for radio and television. She lives in Somerset with her husband and children.

Helen Dunmore was born in Yorkshire and now lives in Bristol. She has been active in women's liberation for several years, mainly in the abortion and anti-rape campaigns. She writes in the mornings before going to work as a printworker at a resource centre. Her poetry has appeared in *Stand* magazine.

Margaret Rodriguez, when last heard of, was living and teaching in Mexico.

Alice Walker was born in Georgia, the eighth child of sharecropping parents. She has written several novels and books of poetry, including *Once*, *The Third Life of Grange Copeland*, *Revolutionary Petunias & Other Poems*, and also a biography for children, *Langston Hughes*. Her most recent novel, *Meridian*, was published in 1976, and a volume of poems, *Goodnight Willie Nee, I'll See You in the Morning*, will appear in 1979.

Judith Barrington co-founded the feminist employment agency 'She Can Do It', was a member of one of the first women writers' groups and was active in the London Women's Liberation Workshop for several years. She now lives in Portland, Oregon, where she is writing, teaching, working for an M.A. in Women's Studies and co-parenting.

Marjorie Jackson was born in Liverpool 'in the days when you didn't talk about that sort of beginning'. She works as a school secretary in Weston-Super-Mare and is married with grown-up children. Many of her stories have been read on local radio, and she has won several literary competitions in the West Country.

Natasha Morgan was born in Wembley, Middlesex. Her first ambition was to be a trapeze artist. She has a baby daughter and works in the People Show, a touring theatre company. Her current ambition is to have a summer holiday.

Rosemary Yates was born in Staffordshire, read philosophy at Sussex University, and now lives in Brighton, where she works in the women's movement and writes.

Dolly Barrett lived in England until her family moved to the US when she was eleven. In recent years she has moved back and forth between the two countries. This is her first published work.

Eileen Fairweather has worked as an actress in fringe theatre and with Melissa Murray co-authored three plays: *Hotspot*, produced by the Women's Theatre Group, *Bouncing Back* and *Belisha Beacon*, produced by Pirate Jenny and Team Two. In 1977 both writers were awarded a New Theatre Writers' Bursary. Eileen used her share to work on her still incomplete novel. She wishes to be known as 'an active socialist and feminist and *very* nice person'.

Anya Bostock was born in 1923, and now lives in Geneva with her two teenage children. She has worked as a translator of Trotsky, Lukacs, Ernst Fischer and Walter Benjamin, and is now absorbed in translating the letters of Rosa Luxemburg.

We have made strenuous efforts to contact all the authors of these poems and stories; we regret very much that we were unable to trace Margaret Rodriguez, Natalia Baranskaya, Nadia Wheatley and Frances Landsman. We hope we will hear from them after this book is published.